READING YOUR NEWSPAPER

By
Larry Parsky, Ph.D.

PARSKY LANGUAGE SKILLS SERIES

EDUCATIONAL DESIGN, INC. **EDI 255**

Acknowledgements

Grateful acknowledgement is made to the following for permission to reprint copyrighted material:

Accu-Weather, Inc.: Weather map and forecast.

Associated Press: "American Embassy in Bogota Attacked"; "Dow Off 0.99 in Apathetic Trading"; "Northeast Growth Falls Behind West."

The Bergen Record: Business Briefs; People in the News; "Insurer Wins Approval to Cover Cats, Dogs"; "Not Run-of-the-mill Day on Hudson Waterfront"; "Schools and a Free Press"; "Shop Owner Clear for Now in Shooting."

Daily News: "Baseball $36M in Red."

Reuters: "U.S. to 'Bill' Honduras."

USA Today: "Car Thefts Up; Midwest Worst"; Car Thefts Chart.

© 1996 Educational Design, Inc. All rights reserved.

No part of this publication may be reproduced in whole or in part, stored in a retrieval system, or transmitted in any form or by any means, electronic, mechanical, photocopying, recording or otherwise, without written permission from the publisher.
For information about permission, write to:
Educational Design, Inc., 345 Hudson Street, New York, NY 10014-4502

ISBN# 0-87694-367-9   EDI 255

Table of Contents

Introduction 4

1. Using the Index 5

2. Reading Your Newspaper 7

3. Newspaper Vocabulary 23

4. The Editorial Section 32

5. The Business Section 41

6. The Sports Section 53

7. The Family Section 63

8. The Entertainment Section 71

9. The Weather Report 75

10. Classified Ads 78

11. Reading Newspaper Advertisements 87

Introduction

To the Teacher

Many of the exercises in this text require your students to locate and comprehend information from a local newspaper. In a classroom setting, instruction will be easier if all students use the same edition of the same newspaper. Most publishers will gladly donate a class set of a recent issue upon request.

To the Student

Successful adult living requires a thorough understanding of many things: money, people, laws, weather conditions, and even ideas. Your daily newspaper is an inexpensive way to learn about these things. It tells you about job opportunities, helps you plan leisure activities, and gives you updates on your favorite teams. It reports on events all over the world that may affect you.

In this skilltext, you will learn how to locate, understand, and use information in a newspaper.

UNIT ONE

Using the Index

❖ Locating Information
❖ Typical Features

10/8/98

Most newspapers have an index, usually on page 1 or page 2. The index is the "table of contents" of the newspaper. It lists the contents with their page numbers. Contents are usually listed in alphabetical order. The index helps a reader find a newspaper feature quickly. See if you can find the index in your local newspaper. What page is it on?

Here is an index for a typical newspaper. This index indicates that the newspaper is organized into sections A through E.

```
                        INDEX
   Arts & Entertainment  E 20-21      National News  A 12-13
   Advice Columns  C 4                News Briefs  A 5
   Amusements  E 25-27                Obituaries  B 17-23
   Bridge  E 25                       People In The News  A 6
   Business News  B 14-18             Sports  C 1-12
   Classified  D 13-26                State News  A 5-6
   Comics  E 22-26                    Stocks & Bonds  B 14-17
   Community News  B 1-3              TV/Radio  E 23-24
   Editorials  A 16-18                Weather  E 28
   Living Section  C 1-10             World News  A 18-20
   Movies  E 21
```

❖ *Exercise One*

Directions:

The index above lists sections by letter followed by page numbers. Using the index, answer the following questions.

Example:

What section and page contain People In The News? (A 6)

1. What section and pages contain the *Sports*? C 1-12

2. What section and pages contain the *Comics*? E 22-26

3. What section and page contain the *Movies*? E 21

4. What section and pages contain the *Editorials*? A 16-18

continued...

5. What section and page contain the *News Briefs*?   A5
6. What section and pages contain the *Community News*?   B1-3
7. What section and pages contain the *Obituaries*?   B17-23
8. What section and pages contain the *State News*?   A5-6
9. What section and pages contain the *Business News*?   B14-18
10. What section and pages contain the *Classified Section*?   D13-26
11. What section and pages contain the *World News*?   C4
12. What section and page contain the *Advice Columns*?   A18-20
13. What section and pages contain the *Arts & Entertainment*?   E20-21
14. What section and pages contain the *Weather*?   E28

❖ Exercise Two

Directions:

Match the correct news item in Column 2 with the index section from Column 1 where it will be located in the newspaper.

Column 1

a _____ 1. Arts & Entertainment
h _____ 2. Classified
e _____ 3. Editorial Page
g _____ 4. Financial
b _____ 5. Home Section
c _____ 6. News Briefs
d _____ 7. Obituaries
i _____ 8. People In The News
f _____ 9. Sports

Column 2

a. A review of a new movie
b. Food recipes and home-decorating ideas
c. A summary of important news events
d. Details about a famous person who died recently
e. The newspaper's view on a particular issue
f. Baseball scores
g. Stock market information
h. Information about jobs, apartments for rent, and used items for sale
i. A story about a person who did something interesting

UNIT TWO

READING YOUR NEWSPAPER

❖ Types of News Stories
❖ News Briefs
❖ People in the News

News! News! News! What in the world is going on? If you read the daily newspaper you will certainly know. Not only will you read about the latest world developments (international), you will also read about what is happening in the nation (the United States or Canada), your state or province, and your city (local events).

The newspaper contains other types of features in addition to current events. You can learn about tomorrow's big hockey game in the Sports Section. You can discover how your stocks are doing in the Business (or Financial) Section. You can decide how to plan your leisure time by reading the Arts & Entertainment Section.

You can add new recipes to your collection or receive advice on a personal problem in the Family and Living Sections. You can look for jobs or a used car in the Classified Section. In the Amusement Section you can enjoy your favorite comic strips and read your horoscope.

So think of your daily newspaper as a kind of bank: it has a wealth of information!

❖ *Exercise One*

Directions:

Match the definition in Column 2 with the term in Column 1.

Column 1

_d_ 1. national
_c_ 2. local
_b_ 3. international
_a_ 4. state

Column 2

a. A news story that took place in a town at the other end of your state

b. A news story that took place in another part of the country

c. A news story about your teacher

d. A news story that took place in Europe and Africa

7

❖ Exercise Two

Directions:

Read the following names of places where an event might take place. Name the type of news event (local, state, national, international).

Example:

London, England   (international)

1. Tokyo, Japan — *international*
2. Your state capital — *state*
3. Washington, D.C. — *national*
4. Portland, Oregon — *state*
5. Your city hall — *local*
6. Bombay, India — *international*
7. Tampa, Florida — *state*
8. Rabat, Morocco — *international*
9. Your neighborhood — *local*

READING THE NEWS

The **front page** is the most important part of the newspaper. Listed at the top of the page in the **banner** is the name of the newspaper, the **edition**, and the date. A large headline in bold-face type describes the major news event of the day (the **lead story**). A picture about the news event is often found below it. The picture usually includes a **caption** that describes or explains what is happening in the picture.

In some newspapers, after you read the headlines you have to open the paper to read the stories. In other papers, the front page itself has the lead story as well as a whole page of other information. What kind of newspaper do you have?

The front page may include articles about all sorts of major occurrences around the world. Each article begins with a headline and then may have a second headline. This second headline is in smaller bold-face type. It describes the article. Beneath this is often a **dateline**. This tells the location of the news story — where in the world it took place. Next is the **news source**. A news source could be the newspaper's own reporters or a **wire service** that provided the information for the story. The major news wire services are:

United Press International (UPI)
Associated Press (AP)
REUTERS
New York Times News Service
Washington Post Wire Service

The story then follows. It answers the following important questions:

Who is the article about?
What did they do?
Where did they do it?
Why did it happen?
How did it happen?

Most of these major points are explained in the *lead*. The lead is the first sentence of the opening paragraph of a news story. The lead introduces the story. The remaining paragraphs provide the reader with more details.

❖ Exercise Three

Directions:

Read the following article carefully. Then answer the questions below.

U.S. to 'Bill' Honduras

TEGUCIGALPA, HONDURAS (Reuters)—The United States will ask Honduras to pay between $4 and $6 million to repair the damage to the U.S. consulate caused by a riot last week in which five Hondurans were killed, U.S. diplomats said yesterday.

"We're going to request that Honduras reimburse us for the damage," one diplomat said.

Even though local governments are responsible for protecting diplomatic property, Washington has, in some poor countries, waived its right to reimbursement for damage.

But it was angry with the Honduran government because police took more than two hours to arrive to calm the riot on Thursday night.

Honduran presidential spokesman Marco Tulio Romero declined to comment on the request, but an official source said Honduras felt it would be obliged to pay.

The embassy attack was unprecedented in Honduras, traditionally the closest U.S. ally in Central America. Twenty-five cars were wrecked, and the consulate was looted and burned.

On Friday the government imposed a 15-day state of emergency in the capital, Tegucigalpa, to quell unrest prompted by what many see as Honduran subservience to Washington.

The embassy attack was triggered by the expulsion of Juan Ramon Matta, a suspected drug trafficker and Honduran citizen, to the United States. Such extraditions are barred by the Honduran constitution.

REUTERS, reprinted with permission

---

1. Circle the lead.
2. What is the dateline? _____
3. List the following information from the lead.
    Who? *Tegucigalpa Honduras*
    What? *The United States will get $4 million*
    When? _____
    Where? *United States*
    Why? *wreckage.*
    How? _____
4. What news agency supplied the story? _____

❖ Exercise Four

Directions:

Read over the news story below. Then fill in the information requested.

Northeast Growth Falls Behind West

WASHINGTON (AP)—The densely settled Northeast has become the nation's second most populated region, falling behind the West for the first time, the Census Bureau reported Thursday.

The bureau also projected that Texas will surpass New York for second place behind California in population by 1995.

And between now and the year 2000, half of all U.S. population growth will occur in just three states: California, Texas, and Florida, the report said.

The projections are based on assumptions about trends in births, deaths, immigration, and movement within the country, bureau demographer Signe Wetrogen explained.

The Northeast has been declining in its share of the U.S. population with less growth than other areas, Wetrogen said in a telephone interview. "It is the one region with the highest share of population in the older ages, and has low birth rates."

Population shifts to the South and West in recent years have drawn away many people in the prime ages of 18 to 24, "so the (Northeast) region is left with more older people, and it's left without anybody to have more kids," she said.

The Northeastern states, relatively smaller in land area than other parts of the country, remain the most densely packed, however. New Jersey leads the nation with more than 1,000 people per square mile.

ASSOCIATED PRESS, reprinted with permission

---

1. Dateline: _____
2. Headline: Northeast Growth Falls Behind West
3. News source: _____
4. List the following information from the lead.

    Who? _____

    What? _____

    When? _____

    Where? _____

    Why? _____

    How? _____

NEWS BRIEFS

The News Briefs Section is an important feature in some newspapers. It gives the reader a brief summary of major articles in the paper. With each summary is the page and section where the article can be found. The News Briefs Section usually contains information about the following categories of stories: International, National, State, Metropolitan, Business, Sports, and Weather.

METROPOLITAN

QUIET ENDING: The controversial murder case that began in 1989 concludes in a San Diego courtroom as a judge dismisses the indictment against Homer "Sonny" Jones.

A-23

STATE

CRASH IN THE DARK: A San Francisco doctor flying a private plane crashed in a hilly section of Marin County early Saturday and was stranded for nearly 10 hours before rescuers could reach him.

A-19

NATIONAL

PRICE TAG ON HEALTH: Americans overwhelmingly like the idea of national health insurance, but only a quarter of them say they'd be willing to pay more than $50 a year in taxes to support such a plan.

A-6

WORLD

SUMMIT POSTPONED: Administration sources say the economic summit scheduled for London in May will be postponed until the fall.

A-9

SPORTS

LAKERS RALLY: Trailing by 15 points with four minutes remaining in the third quarter, the Lakers staged a furious comeback to defeat the Cleveland Cavaliers, 104-102, for their 15th victory in their last 16 games.

C-1

BUSINESS

STOCK PRICES UP: Stock prices were up in moderate trading. The Dow Industrials increased 22 points. The dollar finished up against the yen.

C-1

WEATHER

TODAY: Cloudy, then mostly sunny. Clear and mild tonight; low from 62 to 65.

Complete weather on Page D-12

Index on A-2

❖ Exercise Five

Directions:

Answer the following questions about the News Briefs on the opposite page.

1. Copy the heading used for the article listed in the Business Section.

   _____

2. What is the range of low temperatures predicted by the paper for today?

   _____

3. What two teams played the game described in the Sports Section?

   _____ and _____

4. The economic summit that is expected to be postponed was scheduled for (what city?)

   _____

5. The Business Section summarizes what happened to prices of

   _____

6. What kind of insurance is discussed in the article in the National Section?

   _____

7. Which section lists the article about the 1989 murder case?

   _____

PEOPLE IN THE NEWS

The People Section focuses mainly on famous individuals, like entertainers, athletes, and politicians. Reading about them is interesting and amusing. Here is an example of the People Section.

PEOPLE

SAVED BY THE BAR: Judge **Joseph Wapner** works to protect justice on the "People's Court," but he also inadvertently saved two women from injury. Trossa Fowler, 73, and another woman were taking their teacups to the kitchen in Fowler's home Monday in Port Arthur, Texas, when they stopped to hear the judge. "We weren't really watching it," Fowler said. "But when we passed by, Judge Wapner said something interesting, so we stayed in the livingroom to watch the show." Good timing. It was then that a truck crashed into the kitchen, Fowler said. The 64-year-old driver suffered minor injuries and was arrested on a charge of driving while intoxicated.

FROM HEELS TO HEALING: When the time comes, **Kaye Lani Rae Rafko** says, she'll be ready to "hang up the heels and the tiara and head back to work." But in the meantime, Miss America is promoting her profession, nursing. The 24-year-old former Miss Michigan, a registered nurse, plans to return to a Toledo, Ohio, hospital to work with terminally ill cancer and AIDS patients. In the meantime, she visits hospitals and has spoken to nursing associations and medical groups. She has also done a public service announcement for the profession and appeared on the cover of a trade journal.

MOST POPULAR: Comedian **Bill Cosby** won four People's Choice Awards, while "Fatal Attraction" and its stars claimed three Sunday night in the nationally broadcast popularity poll. **Cybill Shepherd, Dolly Parton, Kenny Rogers,** and **Whitney Houston** also were honored during the 14th annual awards ceremony, which CBS-TV broadcast from 20th Century Fox Studios. Cosby was named favorite male television performer for the fourth consecutive year and favorite all-around male entertainer for the third. He also won a new award—all-time favorite television star—while his top-rated NBC-TV series, "The Cosby Show," won its fourth award as favorite television comedy program. NBC'S "L.A. Law" was the favorite television dramatic program. "Fatal Attraction" was the favorite dramatic motion picture, and its leads, **Michael Douglas** and **Glenn Close**, were named favorite motion picture actor and actress. **Clint Eastwood** was chosen all-time favorite movie star. "Three Men and a Baby" was the favorite comedy motion picture.

The Bergen Record, printed with permission

❖ Exercise Six

Directions:

Read the People In The News feature.
Fill in the following information.

1. a. Name the judge from the "People's Court." _____

   b. Explain how the judge saved Trossa Fowler's life. _____

   _____

2. a. What title did Kaye Lani Rae Rafko win? _____

   b. What was her profession before she won this title? _____

3. Identify the following winners of the "People's Choice Awards."

   a. Name the comedian who won four awards. _____

   b. Name the movie that won three awards. _____

   c. Name the favorite television dramatic program. _____

   d. Name the favorite dramatic motion picture. _____

   e. Name the favorite motion picture actress. _____

   f. Name the favorite all-time movie star. _____

AN INTERNATIONAL NEWS STORY

An international news story contains information that is of interest to people all over the world. It can be about any country in the world. Below is an example of an international news story.

American Embassy in Bogota Attacked

The Associated Press

BOGOTA, COLUMBIA— Two attackers thought to be leftist guerrillas fired a recoilless rifle at the U.S. Embassy on Wednesday night, and an embassy spokesman said the roof was slightly damaged but no one was hurt.

It was believed that two shots were fired and one missed.

The attack occurred at 8:05 p.m.

The two terrorists fled in a taxi, people at a restaurant across the street from the embassy told an AP reporter.

Anonymous persons calling the Bogota television stations Noticiero Nacional and Ultimas Noticias said the attack was by a leftist guerrilla group, the April 19 Movement.

The embassy is in a section of downtown Bogota known as The Bunker, for the elaborate security systems designed to protect the homes and diplomatic missions in the area.

The April 19 Movement, known as the M-19, has claimed responsibility for dozens of bombings against U.S. interests in the last 10 years.

Reprinted with permission

❖ Exercise Seven

Directions: Read the above article carefully. Then complete the exercise below.

1. Headline: _____

2. News source (it appears in a different location from where you might expect it):

   _____

3. Dateline: _____

4. How many people were hurt in the attack? _____

5. Find the following words in the article. Try to figure out what each means from what you read and then write a brief definition. If you are unsure of a meaning, use the dictionary.

   a. guerrilla _____

   b. embassy _____

   c. anonymous _____

6. What is the name of the section of Bogota where the embassy is located?
   _____

7. What is the name of the group that claimed responsibility for the attack?
   _____

UNDERSTANDING A NATIONAL NEWS STORY

A national news story is a story about things in your country. The story shown below is a national news story of interest to people all over the United States.

Car Thefts Up; Midwest Worst

by Sam Meddis, USA TODAY

The Midwest topped the USA with a 9 percent increase in vehicle thefts last year, says a study by the National Auto Theft Bureau.

Increases elsewhere: South, 5 percent; West, 1 percent. The Northeast had a 3 percent decline.

Nationwide, thefts increased 3 percent, the FBI reported this month.

Why the increases?

- More car-theft rings are international, said NATB president Paul Gilliland: "It's not uncommon to learn of vehicles located in South America, Western Europe and Scandinavian countries which were reported stolen in the U.S."
- San Diego's 16.2 percent increase was fueled by illegal aliens stealing cars to go north.
- Detroit's 20.5 percent increase was due mainly to more demand for stolen parts, since people are keeping cars longer.

Some people and companies are fighting back:

- Allstate Insurance this weekend began etching ID numbers on car windows in St. Louis.
- Automakers and insurers are considering a push for tougher laws against forging ownership papers.
- Car owners spent about $500 million last year (a 50 percent increase) on security devices, said John Runnette of Installation News, a trade magazine.

USA TODAY, reprinted with permission

❖ Exercise Eight

Directions:

Read the article on car thefts carefully.
Answer the questions.

1. Headline: _____

2. Find the following words in the article. Try to figure out what each means from what you read and then write a brief definition. If you are unsure of a meaning, use the dictionary.

   a. vehicle _____

   b. alien _____

   c. etched _____

   d. forging _____

3. How much did auto thefts increase in each part of the country?

   a. Midwest _____

   b. South _____

   c. West _____

4. What reason did Paul Gilliland give for the increase in auto thefts?

   _____

5. What has helped to cause the 16.2 percent increase in car thefts in San Diego?

   _____

6. What has been the main cause of the 20.5 percent increase in car thefts in Detroit?

   _____

7. What did Allstate Insurance do in St. Louis to prevent car theft?

   _____

8. What does the article say automakers and insurers want to do to prevent car theft?

   _____

9. Car owners spent about $500 million last year on security devices. What did they spend the year before?

   _____

Auto Theft in 175 USA Cities

Motor vehicle thefts across the USA increased 3 percent last year, the FBI says. Experts estimate losses at between $3.5 billion and $5 billion annually. Listed here are auto thefts for 175 cities with populations of more than 100,000, and the percentage change from the previous year.

City	Thefts	Change
ALABAMA		
Birmingham	3,094	+7%
Huntsville	463	+6%
Mobile	764	-12%
Montgomery	361	-17%
ALASKA		
Anchorage	1,563	+9%
ARKANSAS		
Little Rock	787	-23%
ARIZONA		
Glendale	422	*
Mesa	560	+19%
Phoenix	4,439	-6%
CALIFORNIA		
Anaheim	1,422	+.09%
Bakersfield	856	-3%
Berkeley	782	+16%
Concord	408	+16%
Fremont	350	-9%
Fresno	1,743	+12%
Fullerton	544	-5%
Garden Grove	792	+33%
Glendale	842	+2%
Hayward	401	+4%
Huntington Beach	759	+7%
Inglewood	1,760	-3%
Long Beach	4,171	-1%
Los Angeles	48,507	-1%
Modesto	399	+.03%
Oakland	2,923	+7%
Oxnard	494	+.06%
Pasadena	990	-5%
Riverside	846	-14%
Sacramento	2,235	+11%
San Bernardino	1,070	-7%
San Diego	8.759	+16%
San Francisco	5,783	+2%
San Jose	2,770	+.05%
Santa Ana	1,815	+26%
Stockton	912	+2%
Sunnyvale	256	-10%
Torrance	1,026	-2%
COLORADO		
Aurora	827	+50%
Colorado Springs	924	-2%
Denver	5,022	+4%
Lakewood	499	+9%
Pueblo	283	-5%
CONNECTICUT		
Bridgeport	2,750	-13%
Hartford	1,565	-30%
New Haven	1,621	+9%
Stamford	648	+1%
Waterbury	416	-11%
DISTRICT OF COLUMBIA		
	4,374	+11%
FLORIDA		
Fort Lauderdale	1,776	+8%
Jacksonville	1,865	+23%
Hialeah	1,472	+7%
Hollywood	687	-7%
Miami	5,545	+5%
City	Thefts	Change
Miami Beach	864	+11%
Orlando	684	+11%
St. Petersburg	546	+27%
Tampa	1,721	+8%
GEORGIA		
Atlanta	3,184	+5%
Columbus	560	+27%
Macon	446	-17%
Savannah	522	-7%
HAWAII		
Honolulu	3,099	-20%
IDAHO		
Boise	231	-5%
ILLINOIS		
Chicago	43,635	*
Peoria	196	-4%
Rockford	+330	+9%
Springfield	242	-7%
INDIANA		
Evansville	307	-3%
Fort Wayne	644	+2%
Gary	2,762	+14%
Indianapolis	3,022	+8%
South Bend	387	+28%
IOWA		
Cedar Rapids	340	+4%
Davenport	177	-17%
Des Moines	750	+2%
KANSAS		
Kansas City	1,409	+17%
Topeka	242	-8%
Wichita	977	+.05%
KENTUCKY		
Lexington	707	-3%
Louisville	991	-24%
LOUISIANA		
Baton Rouge	1,049	-8%
New Orleans	5,234	+8%
Shreveport	789	-3%
MARYLAND		
Baltimore	5,415	+21%
MASSACHUSETTS		
Boston 17,219	-2%	
Springfield	1,263	+3%
MICHIGAN		
Ann Arbor	416	*
Detroit	42,505	+20%
Flint	1,520	+65%
Grand Rapids	648	+2%
Lansing	464	+3%
Livonia	641	-24%
Sterling Heights	591	+2%
City	Thefts	Change
Warren	2,131	+15%
MINNESOTA		
Minneapolis	2,145	-.06%
St. Paul	1,087	+3%
MISSISSIPPI		
Jackson	763	+8%
MISSOURI		
Independence	355	-11%
Kansas City	4,338	+42%
St. Louis	5,196	-3%
Springfield	414	-2%
NEBRASKA		
Lincoln	279	-13%
Omaha	1,047	-15%
NEVADA		
Las Vegas	3,008	+7%
Reno	605	-17%
NEW JERSEY		
Elizabeth	1,409	+4%
Jersey City	2,844	-5%
Newark	7.939	+13%
Paterson	1,713	+16%
NEW MEXICO		
Albuquerque	1,622	+10%
NEW YORK		
Amherst	200	+12%
Albany	261	+57%
Buffalo	2,699	-4%
New York	88,478	-5%
Rochester	1,180	-8%
Syracuse	418	+9%
Yonkers	1,488	+4%
NORTH CAROLINA		
Charlotte	1,375	+3%
Durham	312	-18%
Greensboro	314	-16%
Raleigh	580	+50%
Winston-Salem	456	-5%
OHIO		
Akron	977	+17%
Cincinnati	1,102	-4%
Cleveland	13,918	+22%
Columbus	2,665	+7%
Dayton	833	+2%
Youngstown	1,016	-26%
OKLAHOMA		
Oklahoma City	4,152	-1%
Tulsa	4,359	+22%
OREGON		
Eugene	302	-5%
Portland	2,345	-2%

PENNSYLVANIA		
City	Thefts	Change
Allentown	253	+16%
Erie	257	-16%
Philadelphia	13,325	-4%
Pittsburgh	7.677	+48%
RHODE ISLAND		
Providence	3,434	+13%
SOUTH CAROLINA		
Columbia	578	+32%
TENNESSEE		
Knoxville	1,275	-.08%
Memphis	7,927	+42%
Nashville	1,854	+7%
TEXAS		
Abilene	356	+39%
Amarillo	541	-.07%
Arlington	1,324	+33%
Austin	1,687	+19%
Beaumont	575	-9%
Corpus Christi	1,407	+3%
Dallas	8,284	+16%
El Paso	2,711	+25%
Fort Worth	4,158	+18%
Garland	440	+32%
Houston	28,805	-6%
Irving	739	+15%
Laredo	383	+3%
Lubbock	854	+11%
Pasadena	844	+4%
San Antonio	6,937	+21%
Waco	330	+4%
Wichita Falls	399	+7%
Utah		
Salt Lake City	1,100	+7%
VIRGINIA		
Alexandria	632	+24%
Arlington	566	+18%
Chesapeake	231	+28%
Hampton	332	-5%
Newport News	379	-8%
Norfolk	1,105	+13%
Portsmouth	184	-13%
Richmond	903	+.02%
Roanoke	242	-12%
Virginia Beach	578	+9%
WASHINGTON		
Seattle	2,289	-1%
Spokane	535	+5%
Tacoma	829	-4%
WISCONSIN		
Madison	436	+21%
Milwaukee	5,571	+21%

Source: Federal Bureau of Investigation

*No comparable data from preceding years available

USA TODAY, reprinted with permission

READING INFORMATION ON A CHART

A chart can tell us lots of useful information more quickly than if it were written out in paragraph form. Look at the chart on auto thefts. It shows the number of motor vehicle thefts across the United States last year. The chart lists statistics for 175 cities with populations of more than 100,000 and the percentage change from the previous year.

❖ Exercise Nine

Directions:

Answer the following questions.

1. The summary in the box at the top indicates that the estimate of a 3 percent increase was made by

   _____

2. What was the estimated loss from auto thefts?

   _____

3. a. How many auto thefts took place in Phoenix, Arizona?

   _____

   b. Did the number of auto thefts increase or decrease?

   _____

4. Which city in Colorado had 5,022 auto thefts?

   _____

5. Which city in Florida had an 11% increase in auto thefts?

   _____

6. What does * mean? _____

7. Which city in Kansas had the biggest increase in auto thefts?

   _____

8. Which New Jersey city had the biggest **decrease** in auto thefts?

   _____

UNDERSTANDING A STATE NEWS STORY

A state news story provides information about the particular state where the newspaper is located. State news can be of great importance to you because the things happening in your state can have a big effect on your life. Below is an example of a state news story.

Insurer Wins Approval to Cover Cats, Dogs

By Harvey Fisher

TRENTON—New Jersey pet owners can now purchase health insurance for their dogs and cats.

Two policies offered by the Virginia Surety Co. of Chicago were approved Thursday by State Insurance Commissioner Kenneth D. Merin. The annual cost of the policies is $36 or $89, depending on the coverage sought.

Virginia Surety plans to make policy applications available in the offices of most veterinarians in New Jersey, Insurance Department officials said.

This is the first time pet insurance for hospital and medical bills is available in New Jersey. The Legislature and the Governor approved the idea in January.

Virginia Surety's $89 plan provides maximum coverage of $1,000 per illness or injury for a dog or cat. There is a $40 deductible, and the pet owner pays 30 percent of any cost between $40 and $1,000. The $36 policy provides maximum coverage of $2,500, but the deductible is higher—$250. There is a 30 percent copayment, as with the other policy.

The Bergen Record, reprinted with permission

❖ Exercise Ten

Directions:

Read the article above. Complete the exercise below.

1. Locate each vocabulary word in the sentence that contains it. Then write a definition from what you read, or if you must, go to a dictionary.

    a. insurance _____

    b. veterinarian _____

    c. maximum _____

    d. deductible _____

2. Where was this new animal health insurance plan approved?

    _____

3. What company offers the health insurance plan?

_____

4. What is the cost of the two policies?

_____

5. Describe the coverage that a pet owner receives for an $89 plan.

_____

_____

STATE NEWS EVENTS
❖ Exercise Eleven

Directions:

Select an article about a state news event from your local paper. Fill in the following facts about the article. Attach the article to this sheet.

Newspaper: _____ Date: _____

Headline: _____

News source (if any is listed): _____

Dateline: _____

Now write a summary of the newspaper article. Include the following facts: **Who, What, When, Where, Why,** and **How**.

_____

_____

_____

_____

_____

_____

_____

_____

_____

_____

UNDERSTANDING A LOCAL NEWS STORY

A local news story generally has interest only to people who live in the immediate area where the event took place. For example, if a neighborhood baseball team won a local Little League Championship, only a small group of people in the area where teams in the Little League compete would be interested. Below is an example of a local news story.

Shop Owner Clear for Now in Shooting
United Press International

ELIZABETH - Police and county prosecutors Wednesday decided not to charge a store owner with the shooting death of a man who allegedly used a starter's pistol to rob him of cigarettes and about $83 in cash.

The owner, Mohamed Taha, 47, fatally shot Robert Speed, 25, of Newark inside his North Broad Street shop after Speed and an accomplice used the starter's pistol, which fires only blanks, to rob him around 4 p.m. Tuesday, police Lt. Jerome White said.

The case will be presented to a grand jury, which may decide to charge Taha with the killing, officials said.

Speed was found lying on a sidewalk about 100 yards from the store. His alleged accomplice, Thomas Payne, 29, also of Newark, surrendered to police shortly afterward at the urging of his mother, White said.

Taha initially denied shooting Speed but then admitted to the killing after police searched the store and found a .38-caliber revolver used in the shooting, White said.

The Bergen Record, reprinted with permission

❖ Exercise Twelve

Directions:

Read the article carefully. Then complete the exercises below and on the next page.

1. Headline: _____

2. News Source: _____

3. Try to figure out definitions for the following words by reading the article, or copy definitions from the dictionary.

    a. prosecutor _____

    b. allegedly _____

    c. fatally _____

    d. accomplice _____

    e. grand jury _____

4. What did the store owner do to defend himself?

_____

5. What important decision must the grand jury make?

_____

6. Where was Robert Speed found after the shooting?

_____

7. What did Taha admit to the police after they found a .38-caliber revolver used in the shooting?

_____

LOCAL NEWS EVENT
❖ Exercise Thirteen

Directions:

Select an article from your own newspaper about a local news event. fill in the following facts about the article. Attach the newspaper article to this sheet.

Newspaper: _____ Date: _____

Headline: _____

News source (if any): _____ Dateline: _____

Next, write a summary of the newspaper article. Include the following facts: **Who**, **What**, **When**, **Where**, **Why**, and **How**.

_____
_____
_____
_____
_____
_____

❖

UNIT THREE

NEWSPAPER VOCABULARY

This chapter teaches the meaning of 30 important words you need to know to help you understand newspaper articles. These are all words that newspapers use over and over again.

❖ Exercise One

Directions:

The following words are found in newspaper articles about legal matters.

> acquit
> allege
> bribe
> conspiracy
> fraud

Read each sentence carefully and figure out the meaning of the bold-face word. If you are unsure, use a dictionary to find the correct meaning.

1. The jurors decided to **acquit** the defendant because they felt the case against him was not proved.

   To **acquit** means

   a. to find not guilty
   b. to put on trial
   c. to send to jail

2. Several employees **allege** that the customer took the missing watch while it was on the counter.

   To **allege** means

   a. to accuse, to claim something is true
   b. to declare to be the truth
   c. to make a false statement

3. The driver tried to **bribe** the police officer in order to avoid getting a traffic ticket.

   To **bribe** means

   a. to offer someone a gift for doing something dishonest
   b. to pay for your mistakes
   c. to repay a loan

4. The manger found out that the theft was actually a complex **conspiracy** involving six of her employees.

   A **conspiracy** means

   a. a secret plan where people join together to do something dishonest
   b. stealing whenever you feel like it
   c. truth and honesty

5. The real estate company committed a **fraud** by selling people worthless swamp land.

   Fraud means

   a. an honest deed
   b. helping someone less fortunate
   c. an illegal act aimed at tricking or cheating

❖ Exercise Two

Directions:

Below are five more words that are found frequently in newspaper articles about legal matters. Read each sentence carefully and figure out the meaning of the bold-face word. If you are unsure, use a dictionary to find the correct meaning.

>indict
>inquiry
>pardon
>perjury
>probe

1. Grace Fieldstone and her daughter were *indicted* on seven counts of robbery. The trial is scheduled to begin in November. However, the two cousins were set free. The grand jury felt there was not enough evidence to indict them.

   To *indict* means

   a. to accuse of a crime and bring to trial
   b. to get angry in front of the judge
   c. to remove suspicion

2. The airline has begun its own *inquiry* to find out what caused the accident.

   Inquiry means

   a. an investigation
   b. a serious argument
   c. a well-kept secret

3. The prisoner did not commit the crime, so he will receive a *pardon* from the governor.

   A *pardon* means

   a. catching a criminal
   b. escaping from prison
   c. freedom from further punishment

4. Once you become a witness and promise under oath to tell the truth, you had better not commit *perjury*. You can go to jail for lying under oath.

   Perjury means

   a. getting angry under oath
   b. giving correct information under oath
   c. making false statements under oath

5. The insurance company will *probe* the circumstances surrounding the jewel robbery.

   To *probe* means

   a. to ignore the cause of something
   b. to investigate carefully
   c. to keep something secret

❖ Exercise Three

Directions:

Decide which word makes the best sense in each of the following sentences.

  acquit
  bribe
  probe
  allege
  indict

1. In order to win the contract, the company tried to _____ several government officials.

2. The citizens _____ that their Congressman is not representing their interests.

3. The jury could not decide whether to convict or _____ the defendant.

4. The district attorney feels there is enough evidence to _____ the crime suspect and bring him to trial.

5. The investigators for the government plan to _____ thoroughly to find out where all the stolen money went.

❖ Exercise Four

  conspiracy
  inquiry
  pardon
  fraud
  perjury

1. If you testify, you had better tell the truth. Otherwise you might be charged with _____.

2. The customer claimed she was a victim of _____, since the salesperson sold her a vacuum cleaner he knew was defective.

3. The fire inspector made a(n) _____ to find out why the fire spread quickly throughout the building.

4. His lawyers expect him to leave prison soon. They expect him to receive a(n) _____.

5. The FBI uncovered a(n) _____ to smuggle diamonds into the country in the luggage of the members of the team.

❖ Exercise Five

Directions:

Here is another group of words found in newspaper articles.

> abduct
> defy
> denounce
> provoke
> unveil

Read each sentence carefully and figure out the meaning of the bold-face word. If you are unsure, use a dictionary to find the correct meaning.

1. The terrorists **abducted** him from his home in Lebanon.

    To **abduct** means

    a. to bring together
    b. to guarantee safety for other people
    c. to kidnap

2. The striking workers **defied** the judge's order to return to work immediately.

    To **defy** means

    a. to agree to accept
    b. to protect oneself from danger
    c. to resist openly

3. Three more nations have **denounced** the killing of innocent people by the secret police.

    To **denounce** means

    a. to accept a new idea
    b. to plan a revolution
    c. to speak out against

4. The police feared they might **provoke** a riot if they tried to stop the demonstration.

    To **provoke** means

    a. to avoid conflict
    b. to stir to action
    c. to unite opposing groups

5. In his speech on Tuesday, the governor will **unveil** his new plan to reduce taxes.

    To **unveil** means

    a. to disclose or to reveal
    b. to keep a secret
    c. to make not acceptable

❖ Exercise Six

Directions:

Reach each sentence carefully and figure out the meaning of the bold-face word. If you are unsure, use a dictionary to find the correct meaning.

> amnesty
> compromise
> dissident
> quell
> vigil

1. Tax cheats are to be given **amnesty** from having to pay penalties if they come forward and pay their unpaid taxes before next Friday.

    Amnesty means

    a. an award for helping people
    b. a pardon for part or all of the penalties owed
    c. punishment for a crime

26

2. The two women worked out a *compromise* that was fair to both parties.

   Compromise means

   a. a settlement where each person gives up some of his or her demands
   b. a settlement where you convince someone to accept your ideas
   c. a settlement which you are forced to accept

3. A *dissident* picketed in front of the White House to protest the President's foreign policy.

   A *dissident* is someone who

   a. is part of the government
   b. speaks out against the government
   c. supports the government

4. The army can quickly *quell* any uprising.

   To *quell* means

   a. to buy
   b. to march
   c. to put down

5. The protesters each held a candle as they marched up and down in front the governor's mansion in a night-long *vigil*.

   A *vigil* means

   a. a funny happening
   b. a loud cry
   c. a peaceful demonstration

❖ Exercise Seven

Directions:

Decide which word makes the best sense in each of the following sentences.

   abduct
   denounce
   unveil
   defy
   quell

1. The mayor will _____ people who waste water.

2. The CIA learned that the terrorists planned to _____ the prime minister.

3. Several stores plan to _____ the order to close on Sunday.

4. In his speech, the President will _____ his plan for reducing the federal budget deficit.

5. The general said the army can _____ any disturbances that occur during the election.

❖ Exercise Eight

amnesty
dissident
vigil
compromise
provoke

1. The government has arrested the _____ who led the June 9 demonstration.

2. The protesters claim they will not end their _____ until all of the hostages are released.

3. The company will grant _____ to striking workers who immediately return to work.

4. The increase in prices is likely to _____ great anger among the citizens.

5. The two stubborn leaders could not reach a _____ to settle their dispute.

❖ Exercise Nine

Directions:

Read each sentence carefully and figure out the meaning of the bold-face word. If you are unsure, use a dictionary to find the correct meaning.

abide
foil
reject
soar
vow

1. The workers do not like the new company rule, but they will **abide by** it.

   To **abide by** means

   a. to make a big decision
   b. to refuse to do something
   c. to submit to and follow

2. The pilot and his crew **foiled** the hijack attempt.

   To **foil** means

   a. to help someone succeed
   b. to prevent from happening
   c. to send a message

3. If the school budget is **rejected**, there will be no money to pay the teachers.

   To **reject** means

   a. to agree to accept
   b. to refuse to accept
   c. to take from others

4. Shortages of oil cause fuel prices to **soar**.

   To **soar** means

   a. to decrease
   b. to remain the same
   c. to rise sharply

5. Congress and the President **vow** to solve the unemployment problem.

   To **vow** means

   a. to discover a secret
   b. to ignore a problem
   c. to promise or swear

❖ Exercise Ten

Directions:

Reach each sentence carefully and figure out the meaning of the bold-face word. If you are unsure, use a dictionary to find the correct meaning.

    fatal
    impasse
    setback
    immunity
    precedent

1. They were injured but still alive; their seatbelts kept it from being a *fatal* crash.

   Fatal means

   a. avoiding a disaster
   b. causing death or disaster
   c. helping other people

2. The key witness agreed to testify in the drug trial in return for *immunity* from being prosecuted herself.

   Immunity means

   a. assistance
   b. protection
   c. punishment

3. Despite their efforts, the two countries reached an *impasse* in trying to settle their border dispute.

   Impasse means

   a. agreement
   b. deadlock
   c. entry

4. The judge's decision was based on a *precedent* established in a legal decision made in a case from last year.

   A legal *precedent* is

   a. a legal decision from the past that is used as a model for the present
   b. a legal decision that is hard to understand
   c. an old legal decision that a judge disagrees with

5. The rise in unemployment was a *setback* to the President's economic program.

   A *setback* is

   a. an accompaniment
   b. a benefit
   c. a reverse in progress

❖ Exercise Eleven

Directions:

Decide which words make the best sense in each of the following sentences.

    abide
    reject
    vow
    foil
    soar

1. The workers are expected to _____ the company's offer to end the strike.

2. The rebels _____ to fight until the country gets a democratic government.

3. Students must _____ by the school rules.

4. Prices usually _____ when there is a shortage of goods.

5. The army and marines were able to _____ the rebel attack on the presidential palace.

❖ Exercise Twelve

fatal
impasse
setback
immunity
precedent

1. What _____ was there for the judge's decision?

2. Three people were killed in the _____ car crash.

3. The team suffered a(n) _____ when its star was injured.

4. The suspect was offered _____ from prosecution if he would identify drug dealers in the community.

5. The city council failed to approve a new budget because it reached a(n) _____ over how much to raise taxes.

❖ Exercise Thirteen

Directions:

Read each word in Column 1 carefully. Then match a definition in Column 2 with the correct term in Column 1.

Column 1

____ 1. acquit

____ 2. commit perjury

____ 3. abduct

____ 4. indict

____ 5. reject

Column 2

A. Accuse of a crime and bring to trial.

B. Find not guilty.

C. Refuse to accept.

D. To carry off unlawfully.

E. To lie under oath.

❖ Exercise Fourteen

Column 1

____ 1. bribe

____ 2. pardon

____ 3. conspiracy

____ 4. dissident

____ 5. immunity

Column 2

A. A person who speaks out against his or her government.

B. Payment given to someone to do something wrong.

C. Protection offered to a person who cooperates with the law.

D. A secret agreement to do something illegal.

E. Freedom from further punishment.

❖ Exercise Fifteen

Column 1	Column 2
___ 1. fraud	A. Causing ruin or disaster.
___ 2. compromise	B. An investigation.
___ 3. inquiry	C. A plan meant to trick people into losing money.
___ 4. vigil	D. An agreement in which each person gives up something.
___ 5. fatal	E. Staying awake to watch or observe.

❖ Exercise Sixteen

Column 1	Column 2
___ 1. defy	A. To accept, to tolerate.
___ 2. probe	B. To investigate carefully.
___ 3. denounce	C. To increase rapidly.
___ 4. abide (by)	D. To speak out against.
___ 5. soar	E. To resist openly.

❖ Exercise Seventeen

Column 1	Column 2
___ 1. unveil	A. To put down or suppress by force.
___ 2. allege	B. To reveal
___ 3. vow	C. To stir to action.
___ 4. quell	D. To promise or swear.
___ 5. provoke	E. To state as the truth without proof.

UNIT FOUR

THE EDITORIAL SECTION

❖ Letters to the Editor
❖ Political Cartoons
❖ Editorials

The **Editorial Section** reflects the opinions or point of view of the newspaper. This section usually contains **editorials** and **political cartoons** as well as **letters to the editor** to reflect opinions of readers.

Editorials discuss current issues that are often controversial. The newspaper attempts to influence readers to accept its point of view. It criticizes the things that it does not like. It may offer solutions to a certain problem.

An editorial has a **bias**. It is slanted toward one opinion. It does not present both sides of the issue equally. It presents only the newspaper's views. To gain a balanced view of an issue, the reader should read others' opinions in addition to those in the editorial section.

UNDERSTANDING A NEWSPAPER EDITORIAL

Let's examine the controversy caused by a United States Supreme Court decision. The Supreme Court ruled in favor of the principal at Hazelwood East High School in Missouri. It ruled that the principal there did not violate the students' First Amendment rights when he ordered that articles about teenage pregnancy and the effects of divorce on teenagers be removed from the school newspaper. The students, however, had said that the First Amendment of the U.S. Constitution guarantees them freedom of speech and freedom of the press.

There are two sides to this controversy. Here is an editorial that presents one newspaper's opinion. Decide if you agree with this point of view.

SCHOOLS AND A FREE PRESS

By allowing censorship of high-school newspapers, the U.S. Supreme Court did what it had to do. Principals have a right to decide what goes into a newspaper published with school funds. But principals should use this power wisely. Schools need newspapers that are thorough and thought-provoking, just as the rest of the world does.

It may sound hypocritical for adult journalists who cherish First Amendment rights to argue that those rights should be abridged for colleagues still in high school. High-school communities need a free flow of news. Some of that news will inevitably concern drug use, teen-age pregnancy, and other topics that make adults uncomfortable, but those are unmistakable features of the teen—embarrassing problems of school mismanagement that principals want to hush up.

But even adults don't have a constitutional right to see their material in print anywhere they choose. If the owner of a newspaper doesn't want an article published, it probably won't be. No court in the land would interfere. That analogy only goes so far, of course. A high-school newspaper is no one's private property. And the Bill of Rights directly forbids government attempts to interfere with free speech and the workings of a free press.

But school officials argue, correctly, that high-school newspapers are a special case. They are an extension of the curriculum. The newspaper in Hazelwood, MO that figures in the court's decision is published as a part of a journalism class. The school pays for the paper and provides a teacher to supervise its editing. No one would seriously challenge a principal's right to set the curriculum for a class in calculus or literature. That right extends to school newspapers.

If students want to express a personal opinion not sanctioned by the school, they can find another outlet. The Supreme Court ruled in 1969 that high-school students could show opposition to the Vietnam war by wearing a black arm band, for example. Such rights are undisturbed by Wednesday's ruling. But students don't have a constitutional right to air their views in a newspaper operated and financed by the school.

The newspaper, after all, reaches students who may be as young as 13 and as old as 21. They have a wide range of experiences, emotional maturity, and needs. Material that's right for one age level may not be right for another. And the newspaper, rightly or wrongly, will be viewed by many as the voice of the school administration. It's reasonable for administrators to have a right to exclude material that is, in the words of the court, "ungrammatical, poorly written, inadequately researched, biased or prejudiced, vulgar or profane, or unsuitable for immature audiences."

The danger is that the court decision will be used to purge newspapers of inconvenient truths or pictures of the high-school world that don't square with what school officials would like to believe. The school community needs a truthful discussion of real problems as much as any other community. A newspaper is one of the best ways to achieve that goal. But the decision on whether a high school will be served by a real newspaper or a servile puff sheet has to rest with the principal.

—*The Bergen Record, reprinted with permission*

❖ Exercise One

Directions:

The questions below are about the editorial above.

1. Try to figure out the meaning of each of the following words from the context of the article.

    a. censorship_____

    b. hypocritical_____

    c. abridged_____

    d. analogy_____

e. sanctioned_____

f. purge_____

2. Does the newspaper agree with the Supreme Court decision, or disagree?

3. The editorial makes a point of saying that the Hazelwood high school newspaper is published as part of a journalism class. Why is this considered important?

4. a. What decision did the Supreme Court make in 1969 regarding high-school students?

    b. Does the newspaper feel that the new ruling changes this 1969 decision?

5. According to the editorial, what danger might result from this court decision?

6. Do you agree with this editorial?

    Why or why not?

UNDERSTANDING POLITICAL CARTOONS

Political cartoons present a point of view about the news in another way. The cartoon may be created by a staff cartoonist or by a nationally syndicated cartoonist. Political cartoons make comments on current events or issues in the news. They often use *caricature* (exaggeration) to bring attention to a particular point of view. Cartoons also use *satire* (the use of sarcasm and humor) to get their points across to the reader.

❖ Exercise Two

Directions:

Answer these questions about the cartoon above.

1. Do you think this cartoonist agrees with the Supreme Court decision?

   _____

2. Describe how the cartoonist uses exaggeration to express a viewpoint.

   _____

   _____

35

3. Do you agree with the cartoonist?

Explain.

❖ Exercise Three

Directions:

Select a political cartoon in the Editorial Section of a newspaper. Attach the cartoon to the space below.

1. What is the topic of the cartoon?

2. What is the opinion or view that the cartoonist is expressing?

3. Does the cartoon use caricature or satire to get across this view? Explain.

4. Do you agree with the cartoonist's views? Explain.

LETTERS TO THE EDITOR

Letters written to the editor allow readers to express their opinions on issues. A reader might disagree with one of the newspaper's editorials. Or the reader might want to express an opinion about a community problem. Whatever the issue, this feature gives readers the opportunity to express themselves. The newspaper routinely publishes letters that have the broadest appeal to all of its readers. This feature, in effect, creates a public forum for resolving complex problems and features.

Let's see how two readers responded to the Supreme Court decision you have been reading about. Read the two letters to the editor.

Student's Newspaper Has Rights!

The recent U.S. Supreme Court decision supporting the principal's right to censor the high school newspaper is unconstitutional. The First Amendment guarantees the freedom of the press. Since the high school students are citizens, the Supreme Court is depriving them of their basic rights. How can students have faith in our government when they are deprived of freedom of expression?

W. Reed
Cliffside Park

Defending the Rights of Principals

The Supreme Court made the correct decision to support the right of the principal of Hazelwood High School to censor the school newspaper. As the person responsible for the high school, he has a duty to make sure articles that are unsuitable or profane do not appear in the newspaper. Since the newspaper is part of the school curriculum, it should be subjected to the same guidelines as the rest of the curriculum.

G. Michaels
North Bergen

❖ Exercise Four

Which of the two letters above is closest to your viewpoint? Explain.

_____
_____
_____
_____
_____
_____
_____
_____
_____

❖ Exercise Five

Directions:

Write a letter to the editor about the Supreme Court decision that upholds the right of a principal to censor the school newspaper.

1. Use the correct rules for writing a *business* letter. Address it to:

   Your newspaper
   Street address / P.O. Box
   Your city, state, and zip code

2. State your position on the issue. Give at least two arguments that support your viewpoint. Write a complete paragraph for each argument.

3. Write your first draft below. Proofread and edit your letter. Make corrections and changes.

___

4. Write your final draft on a separate sheet of paper.

❖ Exercise Six

Here are some topics that affect us all:

> **Smoking In Public Places**　　**AIDS**
> **Teenage Parents**　　**National Health Insurance**
> **Racial Discrimination**　　**The National Drug Problem**

Can you add other issues to this list?

_____
_____
_____

Directions:

Which of the above topics concern you? Do you have ideas that might resolve some of these problems? Choose a topic that concerns you and write a letter to the editor. The topic can be either from the list above or on some other topic in the news.

1. Use the correct rules for writing a business letter.

2. State your position on the issue. Give at least two reasons to support your point of view. Write a complete paragraph for each reason.

3. Write your first draft below and on the next page. Use correct capitalization and punctuation. Proofread and edit your letter. Make corrections and changes.

_____
_____
_____
_____
_____
_____
_____
_____

4. Write your final draft on a separate sheet of paper.

UNIT FIVE
THE BUSINESS SECTION

❖ The Business Cycle
❖ Glossary of Business Terms
❖ The Stock Market

The Business Section contains articles about the economy, financial management, banking, and news from the world of business. Forces that affect our economy include:

- **Economic conditions.** Are prices increasing rapidly? Is there a shortage of goods? Is the dollar losing its purchasing power?

- **The money supply.** Is it easy for businesses to borrow money? How high are interest rates and mortgage rates?

- **Business conditions.** How quickly is merchandise selling? How much profit is being made from these sales? Are people buying more products made outside our country? Are poor sales forcing some companies to lay off workers?

- **The employment rate.** Is the job market expanding? Or are workers being laid off? What kinds of jobs are available? What kinds of workers do those jobs require? Is affordable training available to those who need it?

- **New/expanding businesses.** A new company in a town or city can mean more jobs, more tax revenues, and more money being spent in the community. Businesses expanding their services or operations can also provide benefits to the area in the same way.

- **Changes in technology.** Some modern technological breakthroughs have produced entirely new industries and thousands of jobs to go with them. Unfortunately, new ways of doing things can sometimes also cause older companies to go out of business. The airplane, for example, has made train travel old-fashioned.

These are very complex economic issues. Some may be difficult to understand. The articles in the Business Section are written to help us better understand issues that greatly affect us. Typical features include:

- A summary of the day's business news.

- Articles that describe and explain major business developments.

- Information about the money supply, interest rates, and other economic conditions.

- The stock market report. **Stock** consists of shares of ownership in large corporations. Stock is bought and sold on the major stock exchanges. The activity of the stock market is influenced by daily business developments.

BUSINESS TERMS GLOSSARY

The following list of business terms should help give you a better understanding of the contents of the Business Section.

Balance of payments	The relationship of the total cost of all the things a country *imports* (see below) versus the total cost of all the things it *exports* (see below). A country has a positive balance of payments if it exports more than it imports.
Bond	A kind of loan. A person who buys a bond lends a sum of money to a company or the government for a specific time. The borrower pays back the money, plus interest.
Capital	Money used to start or expand a business. Also, the things a company owns, such as machinery, tools, and raw materials, which help it make the goods it sells.
Common stock	Shares of ownership in a company.
Corporation	A corporation is owned by its stockholders rather than by a single individual. In many corporations, stock (shares of the company) is bought and sold by the public on a regular basis.
Creditor	A person or group which extends credit or loans money.
Dividend	Earnings paid to owners of shares of stock.
Exports	Goods sold and shipped to buyers in a foreign country.
Federal Reserve System	The central banking system of the United States. It consists of 12 regional banks and is supervised by a Board of Governors in Washington, D.C.
Gross national product	The total value of the goods and services produced by a nation's economy.
Imports	Goods bought from a foreign country.
Income	Money paid to an individual or company for providing some service or product (could include wages, rent, and interest).
Industry	A field of business in which several companies compete—automobiles, electronics, steel, oil, etc.
Inflation	A nationwide increase in the cost of goods and services.
Interest	Money a borrower pays a lender for the use of the loaned money. A corporation, for example, pays interest on its bonds to its bond purchasers.

Interest rate	The percent of the loaned amount a borrower must pay for the use of a lender's money. For example: $80 per year is the interest on a $1,000 bond at an interest rate of 8%.
Investment	Money spent for the purpose of making more money, usually over a long period of time.
Investor	An individual or group which buys stocks, bonds, or real estate. An investor hopes to sell these items later at a profit.
Monetary policy	The regulations of the federal government and the Federal Reserve Board that, among other things, influence the amount of credit available to individuals and businesses.
Merger	The combining of two or more companies into one, new company.
Mutual fund	A company that uses its capital to invest in other companies. The fund sells its own shares to investors.
Profit	Money that remains after all business expenses have been paid.
Recession	A period of slow-down in economic activity marked by a reduction in sales, profits, and employment.
Stock exchange	A place where stocks are listed and traded, bought or sold. The New York Stock Exchange and the American Stock Exchange, both located in New York City, are the two largest exchanges in the U.S.
Trade deficit	A negative balance of payments. A country has a trade deficit if it imports more than it exports.

READING INFORMATION IN BUSINESS BRIEFS

Business Briefs provide the reader with an overview of economic news.

Business Briefs

DURABLE GOOD ORDERS SLIDE AGAIN Orders to U.S. factories for "big-ticket" durable goods fell 1.8 percent in February, but analysts said the second consecutive monthly decline had not shaken their belief that manufacturing will be a bright spot in the economy this year. The Commerce Department report on Tuesday said orders for durable goods (items expected to last three or more years) totaled $111.4 billion in February, following an identical 1.8 percent decline in January.

RATES ON TREASURY BILLS CLIMB Interest rates on short-term Treasury securities rose in Monday's auction, with rates on three-month bills climbing to the highest level since late January. The Treasury Department sold $6.4 billion in three-month bills at an average discount rate of 5.765 percent, up from 5.65 percent last week. Another $6.4 billion was sold in six-month bills at an average discount rate of 5.96 percent, up from 5.78 percent last week.

T-NOTES PLUMMET TO 9-MONTH LOW Yields on four-year Treasury notes fell in Thursday's auction to the lowest level in nine months. The average yield was 7.90 percent, down from 8.33 percent at the last auction on December 23.

MERGER FOR SEVEN-UP, DR PEPPER? The boards of directors at holding companies for Dr. Pepper and Seven-Up have tentatively agreed to merge the privately held soft drink companies, it was announced Monday. The proposed merger is contingent upon the drafting of a definitive agreement and upon obtaining regulatory approval, the companies said in a statement. Terms were not disclosed.

The Bergen Record, reprinted with permission

❖ Exercise Seven

Directions:

Define each of the following terms, either from the way they appear in the News Briefs, or from a dictionary.

a. economy _____

b. interest rate _____

c. durable goods _____

d. plummet _____

e. yield (as in the "yield" on four-year Treasury notes) _____

f. consecutive _____

g. merger _____

❖ Exercise Eight

Directions:

Answer the following questions.

1. In which two months did orders for durable goods fall 1.8 percent?
   _____

2. What was the total amount of orders for durable goods in February?
   _____

3. How much was the average discount rate (interest rate) for three-month T-Bills?
   _____

4. How much was the average discount rate (interest rate) for six-month T-Bills?
   _____

5. a. Name the two companies who are planning a merger.
   _____

   b. What are the terms of the merger?
   _____

READING INFORMATION ON A LINE GRAPH ON TREASURY BILLS

The U.S. Treasury borrows money by selling Treasury Bills, or T-bills, in denominations of $10,000 each. T-bills mature in three, six, or twelve months. The U.S. Treasury pays interest when it sells T-Bills. The interest rate fluctuates.

The line graph below shows how the interest rate on three-month T-Bills fluctuated from January through October.

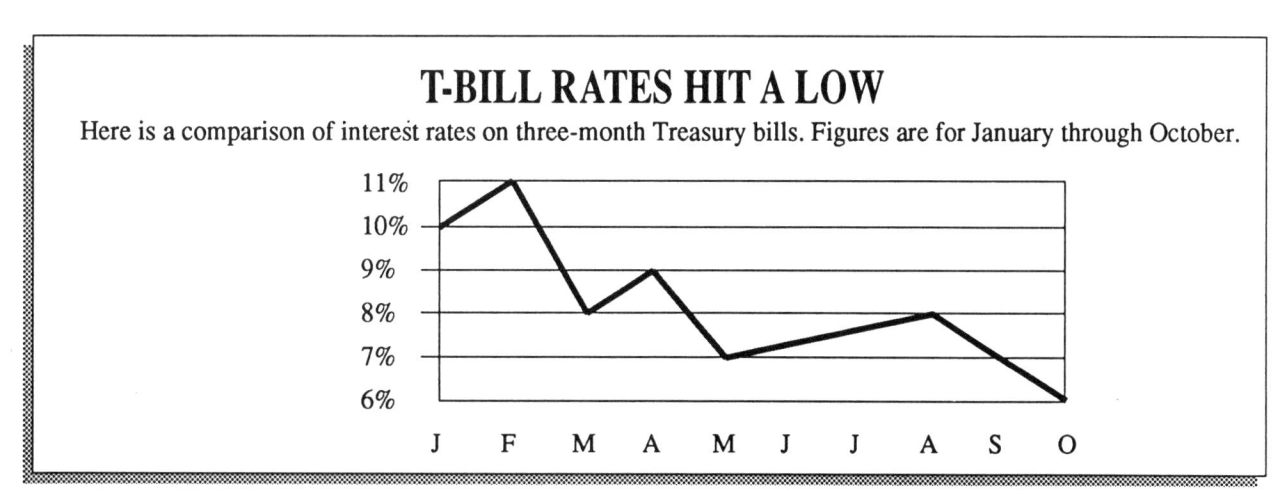

T-BILL RATES HIT A LOW

Here is a comparison of interest rates on three-month Treasury bills. Figures are for January through October.

❖ Exercise Nine

Directions:

Study the line graph on T-Bill interest rates. Then fill in the following information.

1. What do the numbers on the left stand for?
   _____

2. What do the abbreviations on the bottom stand for?
   _____

3. In what month did T-Bills earn the highest rate?
   _____

4. In what two months did T-Bills earn 8% interest?
   _____

5. In what month did T-Bills earn the lowest rate?
   _____

6. What interest did T-Bills pay at the beginning of the year?
   _____

UNDERSTANDING THE STOCK MARKET

Stock market news dominates the business news each day because many people own stock and stock prices are thus of great interest to a lot of readers. The stock market is a place where people can buy and sell *shares* of stock. People who buy stocks are called *shareholders*. Owning a share of stock is like owning a piece of a corporation. If a corporation earns a profit, it usually pays its shareholders a *dividend*. This means that a share of stock earns money. The stock dividend represents a percentage of the corporation's profit.

How much does a share of stock cost? The price for a share of stock for each corporation is different, and the value often changes, or *fluctuates*. How much the stock costs at any particular time depends on what buyers and sellers think it is worth. If the business does well and earns increasing profits, the value of each share of stock is likely to increase. If the corporation does poorly, the value of each share is likely to decrease.

Let's look at the example of Mr. Thompson. He bought 10 shares of stock last year in the Apex Corporation. He paid $36 for each share of stock, or $360 total. The Apex Corporation makes computer equipment. The company's sales increased during the past year and earned a large profit. It will pay a dividend of $2.00 per share of stock. Mr. Thompson made a good investment, since the stock is now worth $42 per share. However, if economic conditions reverse and the corporation's profits decrease, the value of the stock will probably decrease.

THE STOCK MARKET REPORT

The Business section contains the daily stock market report for the New York Stock Exchange, the American Stock Exchange, and the National Association of Securities Dealers Automated Quotations (NASDAQ) National Market. The stock market reports show the daily changes in the value of stock. Here is the latest stock market report for the Apex Corporation.

High	Low	Stock	Dividend	Yield	PE Ratio	Sales in 100's	High	Low	Close	Net change
43	34 3/4	Apex	2	5	10	43	42 1/4	39 1/2	42	+1/4

Here is what this information means:

- During the past 12 months, Apex sold as *high* as 43 ($43.00) per share and as *low* as 34 3/4 ($34.75).

- Based on the last stock dividend, the annual *dividend* is $2.00 per share. This amount provides a *yield* of about 5% annually at the current price.

- The *price/earnings ratio (PE Ratio)* of 10 indicates the price of the stock dividend by the company's earnings per share over the past 12 months.

- On this date 4,300 shares of Apex stock were traded (43 x 100)*(Sales in 100's)*.

- The *high for the day* was 42 1/4 ($42.25) and the *low* was 39 1/2 ($39.50). Apex *closed* at 42 ($42.00), 1/4 (or $.25) per share above the previous day's closing price *(Net Change)*.

ANALYZING INFORMATION IN A STOCK MARKET REPORT

❖ Exercise Ten

Directions:

Find the following information about the stock market in your local newspaper. Fill in the information below.

1. Pick out a stock. What abbreviation is given to it in the listing?

2. List the high and the low price for which the stock sold during the past 12 months.

3. List the annual dividend for the stock.

4. List the yield for the stock at the current price.

5. List the price/earning ratio for the stock.

6. List the number of shares of stock traded on this date.

7. List the high and the low selling price for the day.

8. List the closing price for the stock.

9. List the net change in the closing price of the stock from the previous day's closing price.

❖ Exercise Eleven

Directions:

Look up the following information from the stock market report in your newspaper. Copy the information onto the spaces below.

1. Stock Exchange: New York   Stock: General Mills (Gn Mills)

High	Low	Stock	Dividend	Yield	PE Ratio	Sales in 100's	High	Low	Close	Net change

2. Stock Exchange: American   Stock: Texas Air (TexAir)

High	Low	Stock	Dividend	Yield	PE Ratio	Sales in 100's	High	Low	Close	Net change

UNDERSTANDING INFORMATION ABOUT THE STOCK MARKET

The Business Section usually includes an article that summarizes stock market activity for the previous day. Stock markets have several different indexes to show how certain groups of stock are performing. The changes in these indexes are among the things that are reported each day.

DOW OFF 0.99 IN APATHETIC TRADING

By Rick Gladstone, The Associated Press

NEW YORK - The stock market languished Tuesday and finished narrowly mixed, reflecting what brokers called widespread investor apathy despite another rash of takeover-related buying that boosted some issues.

Economic uncertainty and resilient anxiety about the market were blamed for another slow trading day.

In another similarity to the previous session, the stock market mirrored the behavior of the bond market, a sensitive barometer of the economy's health. Bond prices finished barely changed, reflecting uncertainty over whether interest rates will rise, drop, or stabilize.

The Dow Jones average of 30 industrials, which fell 20.23 points Monday in the slowest trading of the year, vacillated in a tight range and ended down 0.99 points to 2,966.15. Most broader market indicators rose marginally.

Volume on the New York Stock Exchange totaled 142.0 million shares, slightly more than the year's low of 128.83 million shares traded Monday.

The number of advancing stocks narrowly outnumbered declines in composite trading on the New York Stock Exchange, with 765 up, 736 down, and 481 unchanged.

The NYSE composite index of all listed issues rose 0.05 to 151.42. Standard & Poor's index of 400 industrials fell 0.02 to 312.02, and S&P's 500-stock composite index rose 0.10 to 268.84.

At the American Stock Exchange, the market value index rose 0.62 to 298.80. The NASDAQ composite index for the over-the-counter market rose 1.19 to 379.76.

Reprinted with permission.

❖ Exercise Twelve

Directions:

Read the story on the previous page. Complete the following exercises.

1. a. Headline:_____

    b. Writer:_____

    c. News source:_____

    d. Dateline:_____

2. Define each word below on the basis of what you read, or by going to the dictionary.

    a. languish_____

    b. apathy_____

    c. anxiety_____

    d. vacillate_____

3. List two reasons why the stock market performed weakly on Tuesday.
   _____

4. Explain why bond prices barely changed.
   _____

5. Fill in the following information for each stock market index.

Index		
Dow Jones Industrial Average	Close_____	Change_____
NYSE Composite Index	Close_____	Change_____
Standard & Poor's Index of 400 Industrials	Close_____	Change_____
S & P 500-stock Composite Index	Close_____	Change_____
The American Stock Exchange	Close_____	Change_____
The NASDAQ Composite Index	Close_____	Change_____

6. How many shares of stock were traded on the New York Stock Exchange?
   _____

READING INFORMATION ABOUT THE STOCK MARKET

❖ Exercise Thirteen

Directions:

Find an article in the Business Section of your local newspaper that describes the stock market activity for the previous day. Fill in the following information about the article.

1. a. Name of newspaper_____

   b. Date:_____

   c. Page:_____

   d. Headline:_____

   e. Writer (if listed):_____

   f. News source (if any):_____

   g. Dateline:_____

2. Describe how the stock market performed.

   _____

3. Explain the factors that influenced stock market activity.

   _____

4. Fill in whatever information is reported in your article for each of the following stock market indexes.

Dow Jones Industrial Average	Close_____ Change_____
NYSE Composite Index	Close_____ Change_____
Standard & Poor's Index of 400 Industrials	Close_____ Change_____
S & P 500-stock Composite Index	Close_____ Change_____
The American Stock Exchange	Close_____ Change_____
The NASDAQ Composite Index	Close_____ Change_____

5. List the number of shares of stock traded on the New York Stock Exchange.

   _____

READING THE BUSINESS SECTION

❖ Exercise Fourteen

Directions:

Using the Business Section of another newspaper, fill in the following information.

Newspaper_____Date_____

1. List the names of two staff writers or economists who wrote articles for this section.
   _____

2. Which stock exchanges were included in the stock market report?
   _____

3. Copy the headlines for three business articles in this section.

   a._____

   b. _____

   c._____

4. Select a business article with an interesting headline. Write a summary of the article. Include the following facts: Who? What? When? Where? Why? and How?

   Writer or news source:_____

   Dateline: _____

   Summary:_____

   _____
   _____
   _____
   _____
   _____
   _____
   _____
   _____
   _____

UNIT SIX

THE SPORTS SECTION

❖ Creating a Sports Diary
❖ Types of Sports Information

Are you a loyal sports fan? Do you like to keep informed about your favorite teams? Do you look for daily updates about current developments in sports? If you answered "Yes" to these questions, you are probably already familiar with the Sports Section of the newspaper.

How do you feel about the Sports Section of your newspaper? Are you satisfied with the sports writers? Are the feature articles interesting? Are you up-to-date with your favorite teams? The activities in this section will help you evaluate the quality of your newspaper's Sports Section.

The Sports Section is valuable to fans in several ways:

- It has reports about athletic events on the professional, college, and high school levels.

- It has information about team rankings in both professional and amateur leagues.

- It has feature articles about the teams, the coaches, and the individual players and about the excitement and conflict that always occurs in the sports world.

- It may have "Question-and-Answer" columns.

Not Run-of-the-Mill Day on Hudson Waterfront

By Meredith Henry, *Record* Staff Writer

Would Sunday's New Jersey Waterfront Marathon winners be on their way to the Summer Olympics without the 30,000 bottles of Poland Spring Water, 10,000 Del Monte bananas, and 24 bushels of grapefruits consumed by 2,500 runners and a crowd of at least 15,000? Undoubtedly.

With helicopters hovering above and a cheering crowd on the sidelines, Mark Conover finished the U.S. Men's Olympic Trials first out of a field of 100 runners in 2 hours, 12 minutes, 26 seconds. He was followed by Ed Eyestone, then Pete Pfitzinger, both of whom will accompany him in September for the XXIV Olympiad.

Runners in the marathon, which is in its fourth year, covered 26.2 miles in seven Hudson County towns under a gray sky. This was the first time Olympic Trials were part of the event. The Olympic hopefuls were followed on the course minutes later by some 2,500 other runners. The marathon was preceded by a 10K Run, a one-mile Healthwalk, and 100-yard dashes for children.

The Bergen Record, reprinted with permission

N.J. MARATHON WINNERS

U.S. OLYMPIC MEN'S TRIALS:

PLACE	RUNNER	TIME
1.	Mark Conover San Luis Obispo, CA	2:12:26
2.	Ed Eyestone Orem, Utah	2:12:49
3.	Pete Pfitzinger Wellesley, MA	2:13:09

MEN'S RACE:

1.	Barry Giblin Verona	2:38:00
2.	Tim Kearney Culpeper, VA	2:39:07
3.	Ray Renner Maitland, FL	2:40:38

WOMEN'S RACE:

1.	Alma Lopez Mexico	2:46:38
2.	Veta Weir Montague, MA	3:08:16
3.	Carol Johnston New York City	3:10:44

❖ Exercise One

Directions:

Read the above article carefully. Complete the exercise.

1. Headline:_____

2. Writer:_____

3. Define each of the following words from their use in the article, or from a dictionary.

   a. marathon_____

   b. consumed_____

   c. Olympic Trials_____

4. Where did the marathon take place? _____

5. How many runners other than Olympic hopefuls took part in the race?
   _____

6. Identify the winners of the U.S. Men's Olympic Trials.

   Place   Runner   Home   Time

   1 _____

   2 _____

   3 _____

7. What was the distance covered by the 2,500 marathon runners?
   _____

8. What do you think a 10K run is? (If you don't think you know, you might ask some classmates.)
   _____

9. Who was the fastest runner among the women in the marathon?
   _____

10. What was her time?
    _____

BASEBALL $36M IN RED

Major league baseball teams lost at least $36 million last year and are expected to lose $58 million this season, according to figures released yesterday by the Major League Player Relations Committee.

SPORTS PEOPLE

The PRC, which is made up of baseball owners, said that two of the 26 major-league teams had yet to report their financial losses but figures in hand suggest earlier projections of losses were accurate.

These losses occurred despite increases in TV revenues of $72 million. At least 18 franchises lost money.

FOOTBALL: Saints' sale gains

Louisiana's Governor made a dramatic personal appeal to members of the Louisiana House and saved a proposal that gives legislative backing to the sale of the New Orleans Saints. The House voted 53-43 to support the deal and give more than $2million in concessions to trigger the sale. The matter now goes to the Senate.

BASEBALL:

John Tanner overcame a shaky first inning and held Seton Hall to one run the rest of the game as St. John's opened the Big East Conference championship with a 5-3 victory in Bristol, Conn.

GOLF: Four tied in Texas

Mark O'Meara, recovering from jet lag after a victory in Japan last weekend, fired a 4 under 66 that placed him in a four-way tie for the first-round lead of the $500,000 Colonial National Invitational in Fort Worth.

Jim Thorpe, Corey Pavin, and **Willie Wood** shared the top spot. **Robert Impaglia** of the Glen Oaks Club, Old Westbury, N.Y., shot a 36-hole total of 144 on identical par rounds of 72 at the Cherry Valley Club in Garden City and the Hempstead Golf Club to lead 10 Long Island qualifiers for the U.S. Golf Assn. Open regionals June 4 at the Montclair, N.J. Golf Club.

BOXING: Pinklon in pink

Heavyweight **Pinklon Thomas** brushed aside questions about an eye injury and said he was fit and ready to make the first defense of his WBC title against **Mike Weaver** on June 15.

TENNIS: Wilander advances

Top-seeded **Mats Wilander** of Sweden defeated unseeded Spaniard **Emilio Sanchez**, 6-2, 2-6, 6-3, for a third-round triumph at the $435,000 Italian International Championships in Rome. In another match, **Yannick Noah** of France upset No. 3 seed **Anders Jarryd** of Sweden, 6-1, 7-5.

(Compiled by Bill Brown)

The Daily News, reprinted with permission

❖ Exercise Two

Directions:

Read the above sports feature carefully.
Complete the exercise below.

1. Name of writer (you have to look carefully at the article to find it):

   _____

2. a. Headline:

   _____

   b. Explain the meaning of the word "red" in the headline.

   _____

3. Define each of the following words on the basis of the way it occurs in the article.

   a. franchise_____

   b. revenues_____

   c. concessions_____

   d. qualifiers_____

   e. top-seeded_____

4. What does PRC stand for?

   _____

5. What conference do Seton Hall and St. John's belong to?

   _____

6. What did Louisiana's governor do to support his position on the sale of the New Orleans Saints?

   _____

7. Where did the Colonial National Invitational golf tournament take place?

   _____

8. Who does the article say was a victor in a golf event in Japan?

   _____

9. Who will Pinklon Thomas fight on June 15th?

   _____

10. Who won the match between Yannick Noah and Anders Jarryd?

    _____

The sports section includes important charts about your favorite teams. These charts show how many games your team has won and lost. They also show how your team ranks with other teams in its league. Study the following baseball chart.

HOW MAJORS STAND

NATIONAL EAST

	W	L	Pct.	GB
Chicago	23	15	.605	—
Mets	23	15	.605	—
Montreal	24	17	.585	1/2
St. Louis	19	20	.487	4 1/2
Philadelphia	15	24	.385	8 1/2
Pittsburgh	13	25	.333	10

WEST

	W	L	Pct.	GB
San Diego	23	14	.622	—
Cincinnati	22	18	.550	2 1/2
Houston	22	19	.537	3
Los Angeles	21	21	.500	4 1/2
Atlanta	16	23	.410	8
San Francisco	15	25	.375	9 1/2

AMERICAN EAST

	W	L	Pct.	GB
Toronto	27	14	.659	—
Detroit	22	16	.579	3 1/2
Baltimore	23	17	.575	3 1/2
Yankees	20	19	.513	6
Boston	18	22	.450	8 1/2
Milwaukee	16	21	.432	9
Cleveland	15	26	.366	12

WEST

	W	L	Pct.	GB
California	24	17	.585	—
Kansas City	22	18	.550	1 1/2
Minnesota	21	19	.525	2 1/2
Chicago	19	19	.500	3 1/2
Oakland	20	21	.488	4
Seattle	18	22	.450	5 1/2
Texas	13	27	.325	10 1/2

Key: W = wins; L = losses; Pct. = % of games won; GB = games behind first place

❖ Exercise Three

Directions:

Answer the following questions.

1. How many teams are in the Western Division of the American League? _____

2. How many teams are in the Eastern Division of the National League? _____

3. How many games did Los Angeles (in the National League West) win? _____

4. How many games did Boston (in the American League East) lose? _____

5. What percentage of games have the Yankees won? _____

6. How many games is Montreal (in the National League East) behind first place?
_____

7. What team is in first place in the Eastern Division of the American League?

___

STANLEY CUP WINNERS

Annual Stanley Cup winners since the formation of the NHL in 1917 (the 1919 Stanley Cup playoff between the Montreal Canadiens and Seattle was terminated with the series tied at 2-2-1 due to the influenza epidemic). The chart below represents the years from the NHL's beginning to WW II.

1917-18 Toronto Arenas	1925-26 Montreal Maroons	1933-34 Chicago Black Hawks
1918-19 No decision	1926-27 Ottawa Senators	1934-35 Montreal Maroons
1919-20 Ottawa Senators	1927-28 RANGERS	1935-36 Detroit Red Wings
1920-21 Ottawa Senators	1928-29 Boston Bruins	1936-37 Detroit Red Wings
1921-22 Toronto St. Pats	1929-30 Montreal Canadiens	1937-38 Chicago Black Hawks
1922-23 Ottawa Senators	1930-31 Montreal Canadiens	1938-39 Boston Bruins
1923-24 Montreal Canadiens	1931-32 Toronto Maple Leafs	1939-40 RANGERS
1924-25 Victoria Cougars	1932-33 RANGERS	1940-41 Boston Bruins

❖ Exercise Four

Directions:

Study the information in the chart. Fill in the information below.

1. When was the National Hockey League formed? ___
2. Who won the Stanley Cup in 1933-34? ___
3. Who won the Stanley Cup in 1940-41? ___
4. Why was there no winner in 1918-19? ___
5. Why do you think the Rangers are listed in capital letters in this report?
___
6. What is the abbreviation for the National Hockey League? ___
7. Who won the Stanley Cup in 1930-31? ___
8. Who won the Stanley Cup in 1935-36? ___

❖ Exercise Five

Directions:

Locate the Sports Section of your newspaper. Fill in the following information.

1. List the names of at least two sports writers.

   _____

2. List the results of a local athletic event.

   _____

3. Copy the headlines for five articles in this section.

   _____
   _____
   _____
   _____
   _____

❖ Exercise Six

Directions:

Write a summary of one article from the Sports Section in your local newspaper. Include the following facts: Who? What? When? Where? and How?

Headline:_____

News Source (if any):_____

Dateline:_____

Summary:_____

_____
_____
_____
_____
_____
_____

SPORTS DIARY

Do you have a favorite team or players? Do you follow the team's performance? Sports fans often keep a notebook — or diary — of their best-liked teams.

❖ Exercise Seven

Directions:

For this activity, use the next few pages as a notebook. You will read the Sports Section for a four-week period. You will collect articles and other vital information concerning your favorite team. This "notebook" will become your Sports Diary.

1. List the team members on this, the first page of your diary. Include the names of the manager, coaches, and players.

   _____
   _____
   _____
   _____
   _____

2. List the team's game schedule for the next four weeks.

   _____
   _____
   _____
   _____
   _____

3. Keep a log for each game played by the team during the four-week period. Use the following format for each game description.

   Date:_____

   Opposing team:_____

   Where played:_____

   Score:_____

Date:_____
Opposing team:_____
Where played:_____
Score:_____

Date:_____
Opposing team:_____
Where played:_____
Score:_____

Date:_____
Opposing team:_____
Where played:_____
Score:_____

Date:_____
Opposing team:_____
Where played:_____
Score:_____

Date:_____
Opposing team:_____
Where played:_____
Score:_____

Date:_____
Opposing team:_____
Where played:_____
Score:_____

❖

UNIT SEVEN

THE FAMILY SECTION

Is there a section of your newspaper that deals with the home? Is there a section that helps people to enrich their daily lives? There probably is. It is the *Family Section*. In some newspapers it may be called *Life Styles*. In others it is referred to as *Accent*. What types of features does this section include? Here are examples of typical features:

1. **Special feature articles about interesting places.** For instance, a typical article might describe a restored farmhouse that was built over 100 years ago. Another article might be about a charming town that sells unique antiques.

2. **Articles about fashion, sewing, and cooking.**

3. **New and interesting food recipes.** Such recipes add variety to the daily menu. Included could be new entrée items, a low-calorie recipe, or a dessert recipe. This feature is often found in the Wednesday and Sunday newspapers.

4. **Articles about social events.** Typical of such events are parties, dinners and concerts aimed at raising money. These events usually involve wealthy and well-known people in the community.

5. **Engagement and wedding announcements.**

6. **A variety of advice columns.** Examples include personal columns, health-advice columns, and problem-solving columns. Newspaper readers can learn more about themselves and others by reading these different advice columns.

AN ADVICE COLUMN

Problems! Problems! Problems! Life is full of problems. Some problems are easily solved. Others are not. The advice column offers solutions to many problems. Let's find out how a kind-hearted lady helped to solve her problem by writing to advice-giver Ellen.

Dear Ellen:

I am a single person. Not having children of my own, I always made it a point to send my nieces and nephews birthday gifts. Even when money was tight, I always sent a gift or a check.

Well, did my nieces and nephews appreciate my thoughtfulness? In most cases, no. I very rarely received a thank-you note or a phone call. I was just released from the hospital. During the two weeks in the hospital, they did not even visit me or send me a get-well card.

Well, Ellen, it has taken me many years to wise up. From here on, I will not send any more gifts, since it seems I do not rate a thank-you note or even a phone call when I am sick. What do you think?

The Forgotten Aunt

Dear Auntie:

Hurray for you! Throughout the years, I have received many letters about nieces, nephews, and grandchildren who do not have the common sense to write a thank-you letter or make a phone call when they receive gifts. If someone takes the time to send them gifts, they should have the courtesy to find the time to say "thank you."

You are absolutely right to stop sending gifts to your thoughtless nieces and nephews. After all of their failures to acknowledge your gifts, they should definitely be dropped from your gift list!

Ellen

❖ Exercise One

Directions:

Answer the following questions.

1. Why were "The Forgotten Aunt's" feelings hurt by her nieces and nephews?

   _____

   _____

   _____

2. Do you agree with "The Forgotten Aunt's" decision not to send them any more gifts? Explain why.

   _____

   _____

   _____

   _____

LOCATE AN ADVICE COLUMN IN ONE OF YOUR LOCAL NEWSPAPERS

Select an interesting problem from an advice column in a local newspaper. Cut out the problem with the answer and put it in the space below.

Paste or tape advice column in this space.

❖ Exercise Two

Directions:

Answer the following questions about the clipping you picked out from the advice column in your local newspaper. Write a well-developed paragraph for each answer.

1. What do you think caused this person's problems?

_____
_____
_____

2. Do you agree with the advice this person was given about the problem? Explain.

3. Did reading about the problem in the advice column give you a better understanding of yourself and other people? Explain.

A NEWSPAPER RECIPE

Read the following recipe from the Living Section of the newspaper.

BANANA BREAD

4 ripe bananas

1 tablespoon honey

3/4 tablespoon baking powder

2 teaspoons cinnamon

2 1/4 cups whole-wheat flour

4 egg whites

1/2 cup chopped walnuts

First mash the bananas. Then mix thoroughly with the honey. Add baking powder and cinnamon. Now add flour. Beat the egg whites until fluffy. Then fold them into the flour mixture. Add walnuts. Bake in a greased loaf pan in a 350 F. oven for 60 minutes or until you can insert a toothpick into the center and it comes out clean.

Vocabulary

Fold in: To combine delicate ingredients with other foods using a gentle circular motion.

Preheat: Heat oven to desired temperature before baking.

❖ Exercise Three

Directions:

Answer the following questions.

1. What are all the ingredients you mix before you add the egg whites?

_____
_____
_____
_____

2. What ingredients do you beat?

_____

_____

_____

3. What are the last ingredients you add?

_____

_____

_____

4. You have a clock that will ring when you should check to see if the bread is done. How many minutes should you allow before the alarm goes off?

_____

FINDING A GOOD RECIPE

❖ Exercise Four

Directions:

Preparing a new recipe is fun. Locate a recipe in the newspaper that appeals to you. List the following information about it.

1. Name of recipe:_____

2. Name of newspaper where you found it:_____

3. Ingredients:_____

_____

_____

_____

4. Procedures for preparation:_____

_____

_____

_____

_____

READING THE HOROSCOPE

The daily horoscope is another popular feature of many newspapers. A horoscope is based on astrology. Astrology is a study of the supposed effects of the moon, sun, and planets on people's lives. These effects have never been scientifically proven. However, many people still enjoy this newspaper feature just for fun.

Here is a typical daily horoscope from a newspaper. It appeared on April 6 and was meant to guide people in their activities for that day. Read it carefully.

(Note: The dates in parentheses refer to the dates when people were born. For example, if you were born on July 3, you are Cancer (June 22 - July 22).

Your Horoscope
By
Sunshine Sally

Aries (March 21 - April 19). Spend some time today with your family. Take a long walk to ease your restlessness. This is a good time to start a daily exercise program.

Taurus (April 20 - May 20). Use your imagination to overcome a crisis. Save part of your paycheck for a rainy day. You will renew a friendship with an old friend.

Gemini (May 21 - June 21). You must make an important career decision today. Avoid spending large sums of money. Spend some time alone to sort out your feelings.

Cancer (June 22 - July 22). Your boss may seem unreasonable today; don't lose your temper. Make out your own schedule and follow it. Spend some time thinking about your financial situation.

Leo (July 23 - Aug. 22). You must make an important personal decision. Friends and coworkers depend upon you for support. Present your boss with a new idea.

Virgo (Aug. 23 - Sept. 22). Plan an outdoor activity on Saturday. You will receive an unusual phone call. Use your influence to help a friend deal with a problem.

Libra (Sept. 23 - Oct. 23). You tend to have difficulty focusing on projects. Figure out how you can increase your earning potential. You will meet someone important today.

Scorpio (Oct. 24 - Nov. 21). You must make an important decision about a problem from your past. Keep your sense of humor if things go wrong for you. Make sure you follow through on projects.

Sagittarius (Nov. 22 - Dec. 21). A family member will surprise you with good news. You might need more time to develop a personal relationship. Try to see a problem from another person's point-of-view.

Capricorn (Dec. 22 - Jan. 19). You should be in a good mood this weekend. Saturday is a perfect day to spend time with friends. Plan to relax on Sunday.

Aquarius (Jan. 20 - Feb. 18). Examine your long-term goals. You will have support from other people for completing an important project. Share your ideas with your boss.

Pisces (Feb. 19 - March 20). You will be tempted to spend more money than you have. A change in careers could be in store. This is a good time to begin a diet.

❖ Exercise Five

Directions:

Read over the horoscope by Sunshine Sally carefully. Then fill in the following information.

1. What is the astrological sign for the dates between July 23 and August 22?

2. Which astrological sign indicates that it might be a good idea on Saturday to do something like taking a long walk in the country?

3. List the astrological sign that states, "You must make an important decision about a problem from your past."

4. What are the dates for the astrological sign of Pisces?

5. List the astrological sign that states, "You will meet someone important today."

6. What is the astrological sign for the dates between May 21 and June 21?

7. List the astrological sign that states, "This is a good time to begin a diet."

❖ Exercise Six

Directions:

Find the horoscope feature in today's newspaper. Read your horoscope carefully. Answer the following questions.

1. What is your astrological sign with its dates?

2. What is your horoscope for today?

UNIT EIGHT
THE ENTERTAINMENT SECTION

Is it difficult for you to plan leisure-time activities? Are you dissatisfied with the movies you see? Do you find it difficult to find new and interesting things to do? Do you want to attend any future entertainment events? If you answered "Yes" to these questions, you should definitely read the Entertainment Section of your local newspaper.

The Entertainment Section contains such things as:

- A listing with a time schedule for the movies showing in various theaters in the community.

- A review of new and current movies.

- A listing with a time schedule and ticket information for plays, concerts, and dance events.

- A listing of future entertainment events and information about how to order tickets.

- Articles about show business celebrities.

- A listing of cultural events - museums, art galleries, and special exhibits.

Do you know people who cannot find enough interesting things to do?

If the answer is "yes," show them the Entertainment Section. Help them discover how to make the most of the entertainment opportunities in your community.

NATIONAL THEATERS

BARGAIN MATINEES $4.25
Before 6:00 P.M. M-F
First Show Only

$3.50 Senior Citizens All Times.
ID Required

SOMERSET CINEMA
Somerset Mall
745-8166

ACCIDENTAL HONEYMOON
2:00 - 4:00 - 6:00 - 8:00 - 10:00

THE GALAXY MONSTER
STRIKES BACK
2:10 - 4:10 - 6:10 - 8:10 - 10:10

MOONBEAT
1:30 - 3:30 - 5:30 - 7:30 - 9:30

THE MYSTERY OF HOGAN
BAY
2:20 - 4:20 - 6:20 - 8:20 - 10:20

THE MUSICIAN
2:30 - 4:30 - 6:30 - 8:30 - 10:30

REACHING OUT
1:00 - 3:00 - 5:00 - 7:00 - 9:00

OLD ORCHARD CINEMA
Route 4 & Old Orchard Drive
643-2891

MOONBEAT
1:15 - 3:15 - 5:15 - 7:15 - 9:15

ACCIDENTAL HONEYMOON
1:30 - 3:30 - 5:30 - 7:30 - 9:30

VILLAGE CINEMA
Village Mall
472-1032

THE GALAXY MONSTER
STRIKES BACK
12:30 - 2:30 - 4:30 - 6:30 - 8:30

REACHING OUT
12:45 - 2:45 - 4:45 - 6:45 - 8:45

THE AMIGO MAN
1:00 - 3:00 - 5:00 - 7:00 - 9:00

❖ Exercise One

Directions:

Answer the following questions from information in the movie ad above.

1. Name of theater chain.

2. Price of matinee shows.

3. Location of Old Orchard Cinema.

4. Telephone number of Village Cinema.

5. The time the second showing of the "Accidental Honeymoon" begins at the Old Orchard Cinema.

6. The time the last showing of "The Amigo Man" begins at the Village Cinema.

7. The two theaters in the National Theater chain that are showing The Galaxy Monster Strikes Back.

MOVIE REVIEWS

MINI-REVIEWS

Accidental Honeymoon ★★★ (PG). A young honeymoon couple from Iowa are mistakenly identified as spies in the Rome airport by terrorists who plan to smuggle blueprints for a sensitive computer that can blow up oil fields important to the U.S. and Europe. The honeymooners accidentally get the blueprints and are then pursued by the terrorists. Holly Hunter and William Hurt portray the married couple and Allan Arkin portrays the terrorist leader.

The Galaxy Monster Strikes Back ★1/2 (G). Scientists at an experimental space station between Earth and Mars accidentally make contact with robot pirates who terrorize the solar system. The robots learn about the scientists' experiments and plan to annihilate the space station. Outstanding visual effects fail to disguise a weak plot which attempts to copy themes from previous science fiction movies.

The Mystery of Hogan Bay ★★ (R). A sleepy New England town is haunted by a mysterious death of one of its prominent citizens 30 years ago. The daughter of the victim stirs up the town and finds out more than she wanted to know. Jessica Lange's portrayal of the daughter overcomes the weak and unconnected plot.

❖ Exercise Two

Directions:

Find your answers to the following questions from the "Mini-Reviews" above.

1. What do the stars after each movie title mean? _____
2. Which of the movies reviewed had the lowest rating? _____
3. Which movie had the highest rating? _____
4. Which of the movies reviewed is rated R? _____
5. Which of the movies reviewed stars Holly Hunter and William Hurt? _____
6. Which movie has outstanding visual effects? _____
7. Which movie stars Jessica Lange? _____
8. Would any of these movies appeal to you? _____
   If so, which one(s)? _____

❖ Exercise Three

Directions:

Locate the Entertainment Section in your local newspaper. Fill in the following information.

1. On what pages(s) is the Entertainment Section located?_____

2. List the following information for a movie that you want to see.

   a. Name of movie:_____

   b. Theater:_____

   c. Today's time schedule:_____

3. List the name of a movie that is reviewed in the newspaper.

   _____

4. Describe the review.

   _____

   _____

   _____

   _____

5. What is the newspaper's rating for the movie?_____

6. List the following information for a play, concert, or dance event that you might want to see.

   Name of event:_____

   Theater:_____

   Time:_____Price of ticket:_____

7. List the headline for an article about an entertainer.

   _____

8. Give a brief summary of the article. (Include the following facts: Who - What - When - Where - Why - and How.)

   _____

   _____

   _____

   _____

UNIT NINE

THE WEATHER REPORT

❖ Reading a Weather Map
❖ Glossary of Weather Terms

The *Weather Report* helps us plan our daily activities. It describes the local, national, and "extended" (future) forecasts. It also tells us about unusual trends and events, like floods and earthquakes.

Special words are used to explain the weather. Here is a list of key terms.

Forecast	A prediction of coming weather conditions.
Foreign	Located outside our country.
Humidity	The amount of moisture and dampness in the air.
Mean	An average (as in "mean—meaning average—temperatures").
Metropolitan	A city and its surrounding area within a 30-mile radius.
National	Relating to the entire country.
Pollution	Dirty air caused by smoke, carbon monoxide, and other chemicals.
Precipitation	The depositing of rain, snow, and sleet on the earth.
Tides	The periodic rise and fall of the oceans, caused by the attraction of the sun and moon.
Wind chill factor	The effect of wind on temperatures. The wind makes the air feel colder than it actually is.

ACCU-WEATHER ®

Local Forecast
Mostly cloudy today with occasional drizzle and a few showers. High 65-70. An evening shower, then gradual clearing tonight. Low 48-53.

Five-Day Forecast
TODAY: Mostly cloudy, occasional rain, a few showers. High 70, low 52.
TOMORROW: Mostly sunny, breezy, and pleasant. High 72, low 52.
SATURDAY: Mainly sunny and warm. High 78, low 56.
SUNDAY: Mixture of clouds and sun, warm, slight chance of thundershower. High 78, low 56.
MONDAY: Variable cloudiness, chance of a shower. High 76, low 58.

Today's Highs—Tonight's Lows

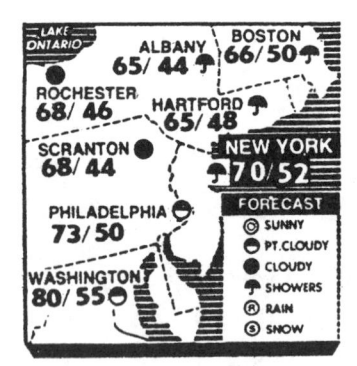

ALBANY 65/44
BOSTON 66/50
ROCHESTER 68/46
HARTFORD 65/48
SCRANTON 68/44
NEW YORK 70/52
PHILADELPHIA 73/50
WASHINGTON 80/55

FORECAST
- SUNNY
- PT.CLOUDY
- CLOUDY
- SHOWERS
- RAIN
- SNOW

National Summary
Showers and thunderstorms will occur in portions of the Northeast as well as south Texas. Showers will affect portions of the northern Plains states, and rain and snow showers will occur in the Rockies. The highest elevations of the Rockies will pick up a few inches of wet snow. The remainder of the country will enjoy dry conditions.

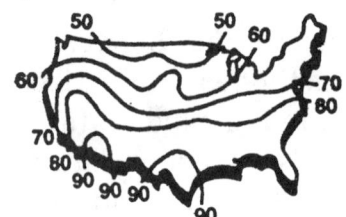

Temperature in New York
Wednesday's Max. 53 at 3:45 p.m.
Wednesday's Min. 49 at 2:50 a.m.
Highest April 24, 83 in 1866.
Lowest April 24, 31 in 1930.
Mean temperature 51; normal, 55; average temperature departure since April 1, +2.58. Degree days April 23, 11 since July 1, 4141; last year to date, 4686, normal to date 4676.

Precipitation
Yesterday, 0.00; total since April 1, 1.31; total since January 1, 6.63 inches; normal since January 1, 13.33 inches; last year to this date, 17.04 inches.

Temp./Humidity Index
Yesterday
8 a.m. 49, noon 52, 4 p.m. 54.
Today
8 a.m. 56, noon 64, 4 p.m. 70.

Pollution Forecast
Air quality will be moderate today and good tomorrow.

Tides
	High		Low	
	a.m.	p.m.	a.m.	p.m.
Barnegat In.	10:40	10:45	4:39	4:18
Sandy Hook	11:01	11:06	4:58	4:37
Battery	11:33	11:38	5:22	4:51
Willet's Pt.	1:46	2:22	8:22	8:31
Stamford	2:05	2:38	8:38	8:47
Fire Is. In.	10:21	10:26	4:09	3:48
Montauk Pt.	10:50	11:38	5:51	5:44

Sun, Moon and Planets
Sun rises in New York 5:03 a.m., sets 6:46 p.m., rises tomorrow 5:02 a.m., sets 6:47 p.m. Moon rises 8:16 a.m., sets ____ Morning planets: Venus, Jupiter, Mercury, Saturn. Evening Planets: Mars.

Apr. 20   Apr. 27   May 4   May 11
●   ◐   ○   ◑
New   First Q. Full   Last Q.

U.S. Cities

City	Today	Tomorrow
Albany	65/44sh	68/44pc
Atlanta	83/58s	83/60s
Atlantic City	66/50sh	72/52s
Boston	66/50sh	70/50pc
Chicago	70/50s	70/54s
Cleveland	68/46s	68/46s
Dallas	86/63s	84/63pc
Denver	82/39sh	40/35r
Detroit	68/46s	70/48pc
Honolulu	84/70s	84/70pc
Houston	86/62s	86/64pc
Kansas City	73/58pc	70/58c
Las Vegas	77/50pc	72/46pc
Los Angeles	72/54pc	70/52pc
Miami	82/69pc	82/70pc
Minneapolis	63/43pc	60/40pc
New Orleans	85/68s	87/72s
Orlando	88/66pc	88/66pc
Phoenix	90/60s	83/57pc
Philadelphia	73/50pc	73/50s
Pittsburgh	70/46pc	76/50s
Portland	56/43pc	60/43c
Salt Lake City	49/32sh	48/30c
San Francisco	65/44s	67/46c
San Juan	85/72pc	85/72pc
Washington	80/55pc	80/52s

Foreign Cities

City	Today	Tomorrow
Athens	68/50pc	72/52s
Berlin	46/34sh	48/30pc
Cairo	83/65s	85/63s
Dublin	54/38c	51/32pc
Jerusalem	70/43s	77/64s
London	53/36s	50/30pc
Madrid	62/44c	64/42c
Montreal	66/48c	60/40pc
Moscow	58/45sh	54/40sh
Ottawa	65/45c	62/40c
Paris	56/33pc	50/36c
Rome	60/44c	64/46c
Stockholm	45/30c	43/29c
Tokyo	67/52pc	70/50pc
Warsaw	45/32c	45/29c

Key to Codes
S Sunny   PC Partly cloudy
C Cloudy SH Showers
R Rain   T Thunderstorms
I Ice   SF Snow flurries

reprinted with permission

❖ Exercise One

Directions:

Study the preceding weather report carefully. Then answer the following questions.

1. Referring to the Five-Day Forecast, what is the prediction for —

   a. Tomorrow?_____

   b. Saturday?_____

2. What was the maximum temperature in New York on Wednesday?

_____

3. Draw the following symbols as they appear on the weather map:

   sunny   cloudy   rain

4. What do the following abbreviations mean (lower right)?

   S_____ PC_____

5. How much precipitation was there yesterday?_____

6. List the following precipitation information.

   a. Total since April 1:_____

   b. Total since January 1:_____

   c. Normal since January:_____

   d. Total last year to this date:_____

THE WEATHER REPORT
❖ Exercise Two

Directions:

Using today's newspaper, answer these questions about the weather.

1. On what page is the weather report located?_____

2. What is the local or metropolitan area weather forecast?

   _____

3. How much precipitation was there yesterday?_____

4. Is there an extended forecast? _____ For how many days?_____

5. What is the prediction for tomorrow's weather in Moscow? _____

   Rome?_____

❖

UNIT TEN

CLASSIFIED ADS

❖ Types of Classified Ads
❖ Understanding Abbreviations
❖ Answering Ads

The Classified Section is often called "the people's marketplace." It allows people to buy or sell goods, find employment, locate houses or apartments, and place announcements. The Classified Section brings together sellers and buyers. It also unites job seekers with employers.

Here are the types of classified ads to be found in this section:

- Cars, Trucks, and Other Vehicles
- Personals/Announcements
- Help Wanted
- Instruction
- Business Opportunities
- Pets
- Merchandise for Sale
- Apartments/Houses for Rent
- Real Estate

Study the following ads:

> RETAIL: GROW WITH US!
> Exc. opptys for career-minded indiv. w/home furn. chain. F/T perm. pos. open for exp. Sales, Stock, Cashiers & Asst. Mgr. Trainees. Co. Pd. Benfts. M/F non-smokers prf'd. 344-0954 10–8:30 daily. EOE

> Salesperson wtd. w/exp. in selling wallpaper. F/T. Call Mr. Adams 231-1211

> SPRINGVIEW PARK. 3 Bdrm., bsm. gar., $185,000. Beautiful! Elk Realty. Call Ms. Nunez, 482-1921

Some words in the above ads are abbreviated. Words are abbreviated mainly to save space. Here is a key for some of those words:

Abbreviation	Word	Abbreviation	Word
adv.	advancement	nec.	necessary
exp.	experienced	ph.	phone
co.	company	mo.	month(ly)
bnft.	benefits	oppty.	opportunity
appt.	appointment	sal.	salary
f/t	full time	bedr.	bedroom
immed.	immediately	gar.	garage
wpm	words per minute	min.	minimum
mgr.	manager(ial)	ref.	reference(s)
asst.	assist(ant)	perm.	permanent
exc.	excellent	pref'd	preferred
qual'd	qualified	w.p.	word processor
req'd	required	gd.	good

❖ *Exercise One*

Directions:

Rewrite the classified ads on the previous page in the space below. Write out the complete word for each abbreviated word.

1. _____

2. _____

3. _____

❖ Exercise Two

Directions:

Write out possible abbreviations for each of the following words or phrases used in Want Ads:

1. words per minute _____
2. part time _____
3. monthly _____
4. living room _____
5. restaurant _____
6. opportunity _____
7. student _____
8. high school graduate _____
9. extension _____
10. telephone _____
11. high floor _____
12. agent _____
13. negotiate _____
14. Tuesday _____
15. Sunday _____

❖ Exercise Three

Directions:

Write out the full meaning of the following abbreviations:

1. no exp. nec. _____
2. gd. oppty. for adv. _____
3. 5 BR, 3 Bth _____
4. exc. med. bnft. _____
5. ph. for appt. _____
6. sal. neg. _____

❖ Exercise Four

Directions:

Read over the want ads below. Rewrite each one on the lines provided, using abbreviations whenever possible.

1. Gas attendants: Full/Part time, days/nights/weekends. Earn up to $6 per hour. Call 325-1524. Ask for Bill Blandy.

2. Gal/Guy Friday: Stock work. No experience necessary. Full time, good benefits. Call Mr. Martinez at 982-2311 between 9-5.

3. Dental Assistant. Will train mature person. No experience necessary. Typing skills required. Position available immediately. Call 584-2130 between 10 a.m. - 2:30 p.m., Monday through Friday.

4. Cashier needed to work part time, evenings and Saturdays. Experience not required. Call Greg between 10-4, 432-9145.

5. Receptionist. Good phone skills, typing, sixty words per minute. Opportunity for advancement. Excellent salary and benefits. Call Ms. Rodgers at 974-2100.

❖ *Exercise Five*

OPEN HOUSE

Wednesday and Thursday,
May 22 and 23, from 5PM-8PM

We're currently hiring for the following positions:

- WORD PROCESSORS
- CLERK TYPIST
- DATA ENTRY
- OPERATORS
- ACCOUNTS PAYABLE
- CLERKS
- FILE CLERKS
- SECRETARIES

As one of the largest toy retailers in the world, we offer competitive salaries and even benefits where applicable. Be sure to come to our Open House being held at our headquarters:
1200 North High Street, Hackensack, New Jersey 07662

Just call and ask for directions.

TOYS UNLIMITED
201-555-3300
An Equal Opportunity Employer

Directions:

Read the help-wanted ad above. Fill in the following information:

1. Name of company:_____

2. Address:_____

3. Type of business:_____

4. When the Open House is scheduled (dates and times):_____

5. Types of positions available (list three):_____

6. How to get additional information:_____

7. Explain the following statement: "We offer competitive salaries..."

    _____

    _____

8. Explain the phrase *An Equal Opportunity Employer*.

    _____

    _____

❖ *Exercise Six*

Charter Oaks Gardens

Spacious 1, 2 & 3 BR APTS.
Includes heat, hot water, & A/C
Starting from $775 per month

(615) 555-4055

Directions: River Parkway to Exit 116
Take Route 36 approximately 10 miles to
Charter Oaks Gardens on the left.

Directions:

Read the information carefully in the above advertisement for an apartment. Fill in the information below about this ad.

1. Name of apartment complex:_____

2. Description of apartments given in ad:

   _____

   _____

3. What does the ad say about rents?

   _____

4. What does the ad mean when it describes rents as starting from $775 per month?

   a. all apartments cost this
   b. $775 is the average
   c. some cost more

5. Telephone number for getting addition information:

   _____

83

6. Directions for getting to this apartment complex.

_____
_____
_____

❖ Exercise Seven

MERCURY COUGAR LS

Auto Trans, ODrive, 3.6 E.F.I. V-6, Power Steering, Brakes & Windows, R/W Def, Tilt Wheel, Cruise, Cassette, Clear Coat Paint, stk #990306

LIST PRICE $16,749
SAVE 3,000
BUY FOR $13,749

36 Month Red Carpet Lease At $245 per mo.

★★★★★
STAR MERCURY

1505 TELEGRAPH ROAD
(NEAR TWELVE MILE ROAD)
Phone: 823-1400
Showroom open MON-FRI
9:00 A.M. - 9:00 P.M.
SAT - 9:00 A.M. - 5:00 P.M.
★★★★★

Directions:

Read over the information in the above advertisement for an automobile. Then fill in the information below about this ad.

1. Name of car:_____

2. List the equipment that is included on this automobile.

_____
_____
_____
_____

3. List price of automobile:

   _____

4. Amount deducted from list price:

   _____

5. Final selling price of automobile:

   _____

6. Leasing information: _____ months at $_____ per month

   Total leasing cost for 36 months (multiply):_____

7. List the following information about the car dealer:

   Name_____

   Address_____

   Telephone number_____

❖ Exercise Eight

Directions:

Use a current newspaper to find the following information in the Classified Section.

1. List the pages where the Classified Section is located._____

2. Describe the type of information that is found in this section.

   _____

   _____

   _____

3. Find a help-wanted ad for a job that interests you. List the important information from this ad.

   _____

   _____

   _____

4. Find a help-wanted ad for a word processing or secretarial job. List the important information from this ad.

_____

_____

_____

5. List important information for a used-car or used-furniture item.

_____

_____

_____

6. List information for an unfurnished rental apartment.

_____

_____

❖

UNIT ELEVEN
Reading Newspaper Advertisements

Regular newspaper advertisements, or "ads," are an important part of the newspaper. They often provide important information about goods and services that are available in the community. They show newspaper readers which stores sell the products they need. They let shoppers know about new products. And they often list special store sales where readers may be able to save money.

Do you read newspaper ads? Do ads help you to find information about the products you need? Do ads help you discover new products? The activities in this section will teach you to analyze ads more critically. This will help you become a better shopper.

UNDERSTANDING THE INFORMATION IN AN ADVERTISEMENT FOR A PRODUCT

Among the most common types of advertisements you find in newspapers are retail (store) ads listing products for sale. These ads usually contain a lot of useful information — information that can help consumers make their buying decision. But such ads have to be read very carefully.

SUPER SALE!!!
TRACY'S DEPARTMENT STORE

AT ALL OUR LOCATIONS:
- HUDSON MALL
- OAKLAND MALL
- 3000 WEST 34th STREET
- RIVERSIDE SQUARE
- ORCHARD MALL
- 1540 WOODWARD AVENUE

SAVE $103

19-inch cable compatible color TV with remote
- 117 channel cable-compatible quartz tuner
- Convenient 17-key remote with off-timer
- Sharpness control
- 19-in. diagonal measure color picture
- Model #7100

$296
Reg. $399.99

ORDER BY PHONE: 555-4833
SALE STARTS WEDNESDAY, July 31
SALE ENDS, SATURDAY, August 3
STORE HOURS: MONDAY THRU SATURDAY - 10:00 A.M. til 9:30 P.M.
SUNDAY: 12:00 P.M. til 5:30 P.M.

❖ Exercise One

Directions:

Read over the store advertisement on the previous page and fill in the following information about it.

1. Name of store: _____

2. Locations: _____
   _____
   _____

3. Store hours: _____
   _____

4. Type of product being advertised:
   _____

5. Features of this product:
   _____
   _____
   _____
   _____

6. Model number: _____

7. Regular price: _____ Sale price: _____

8. Dates of the sale:
   _____
   _____

9. What is the number for ordering this product by phone? _____

10. Explain how this ad might help a consumer who wants to buy a television set.
    _____
    _____
    _____
    _____
    _____

CAPITAL ELECTRONICS, INC.

WILLOW BROOK MALL - Route 3 and Willow Brook Drive
Phone: 555-7255
OPEN 7 DAYS A WEEK - Mon-Sat - 10:00-9:30, Sun - 11:00-5:00

SAVE $50 . . . JVC PORTABLE COMPONENT STEREO
Sale $119
Orig. $169
U-turn auto-reverse stereo cassette recorder, hyper bass sound system, AM/FM stereo tuner, 5 band graphic equalizer, detachable speakers with 4" drivers. Model #PCV55.

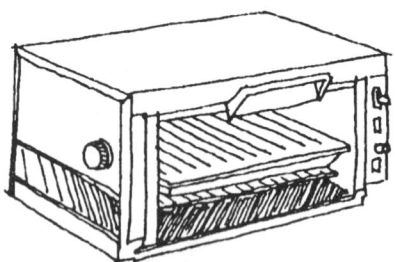

SONY TR-5
Sale $888
Sony's Smallest 8mm Camcorder with Autofocus & Zoom Lens. Complete with all Sony accessories and Sony USA Warranty. Originally $950.
ACCESSORIES INCLUDE:
- BATTERY
- AC POWER ADAPTOR
- BATTERY CHARGER
- RF CONVERTER

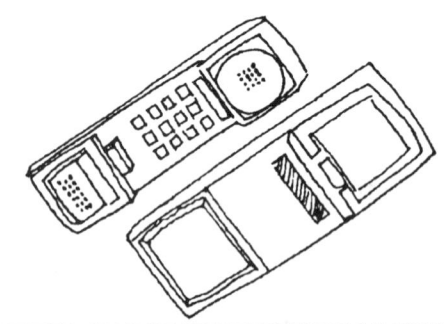

SAVE 33% AFTER REBATE. . . PROCTOR-SILEX R CONTINUOUS CLEAN TOASTER OVEN/BROILER
Originally $45 ....$40
Less Mfgr's Mail-in Rebate ....-$10
FINAL COST $30
Temperature range from keep warm to broil. Costs less to operate than a conventional oven. 4 slice toasting with shade selector. Model #0245.

GE TRIMLINE EXTENSION PHONE
Sale $19.99
With tone/pulse dialing, fully lighted keypad. Desk or wall mountable. Available in choice of assorted colors. Orig. $24.99 Model #9110.

Charge purchases with your Visa Card or MasterCard

❖ Exercise Two

Directions:

Read the store advertisement on the previous page carefully. Then answer the following questions.

1. Name of store:_____

2. Location:_____

3. Phone:_____

4. Store hours:_____

5. JVC Portable Component Stereo

   A. Describe the features of this product.

   _____

   _____

   _____

   _____

   B. Model number:_____

   C. Original price:_____Sale price:_____

6. Proctor-Silex Continuous Clean Toaster Oven/Broiler

   A. Describe the features of this product.

   _____

   _____

   _____

   _____

   B. Model number:_____

   C. Original price:_____Sale price (before mfgr's rebate):_____

   Manufactures mail-in rebate:_____Final cost:_____

   D. Explain what a manufacturer's rebate is.

   _____

   _____

7. Sony 8mm Camcorder

   A. Describe the features of this product.

   _____

   _____

   _____

   _____

   B. Model number:_____

   C. Does this product come with a warranty? _____

   Explain what this means.

   _____

   _____

   D. Original price:_____Sale price:_____

8. GE Trimline Extension Phone

   A. Describe the features of this product.

   _____

   _____

   _____

   _____

   B. Model number:_____

   C. Original price:_____Sale price:_____

9. Which credit cards can a customer use to buy products from this store?

   _____

UNDERSTANDING THE INFORMATION ON A STORE COUPON

Friendly Supermarkets Coupon

6 1/2 oz. can Fancy Albacore White in oil or water

Star-Kist Solid Tuna 89¢

AS SEEN ON TV

Limit one per family.
Good at any Friendly Supermarket,
Sun., May 12 thru Sat., May 18,
Offer void where prohibited

❖ Exercise Three

Directions:

Special product coupons like the one above sometimes are included in store ads. Fill in the information below about this coupon.

1. Name of supermarket chain:_____
2. Name of product:_____
3. Type of tuna fish:_____
4. Size of product:_____
5. Choices of liquid for which the product is available:_____
6. Price of product with coupon:_____
7. How many cans can a family buy on the special coupon offer?_____
8. Where can this coupon be used?_____
9. Dates when this coupon can be used:_____
10. Explain what the following statement means: "Offer void where prohibited."

_____
_____
_____

UNDERSTANDING THE INFORMATION IN A SUPERMARKET AD

FRIENDLY SUPERMARKETS
OPEN 24 HOURS—7 DAYS

FRESH DAILY PRODUCTS

Orange Juice	Pure Premium, Reg. or Homestyle, Tropicana, 1/2 gal. cart.	**$2.89**
Fruit Punch	or Lemonade, Tropicana 1/2 gal. cont.	**99¢**
Juice Blends	Tropicana Grapefruit, Pineapple, Grapefruit, or Orange Pineapple 1/2 gal. cart.	**$2.29**
Tropicana Juice	Orange-Strawberry-Banana 1/2 gal. cart.	**$2.29**
Whipped Butter	Breakstone's Lightly Salted or Sweet, 8 oz. cont.	**99¢**
Sour Cream	or Light Choice, Breakstone's 16 oz. cont.	**99¢**
Temp Tee	Whipped Cream Cheese 8 oz. cont.	**$1.29**

FRESH MEATS

Turkey Breast	Hotel Style, Shady Brook Farms Wings, Necks, and Giblets	**$1.19**
Ground Turkey	Fresh, Shady Brook	**$1.99**
Turkey Sausage	Italian, Sweet, Fresh Shady Brook	**$1.99**
Turkey Cutlets	Fresh, Shady Brook	**$3.49**
Drumsticks	and Wings, Turkey, Shady Brook, Fresh	**89¢**
Turkey Sausage	Fresh, Hot Italian Shady Brook	**$1.99**

FRESH PRODUCE

LOW IN CALORIES, SUPER SELECT
Fresh Cucumbers — 3 for 1.00
LOW IN CALORIES
Pascal Celery — .79 ea.
ESCAROLE, CHICORY OR
Romaine Lettuce — .69 / lb.
HIGH IN IRON
Fresh Spinach 10-oz. bag — 1.29
IMPORTED FROM ISRAEL
Fresh Tomatoes — 1.99 / lb.

VERY LOW CALORIES, IMPORTED 6 SIZE
Honeydew Melons — 2.99 ea.
PLUMP AND SWEET
Red Raspberries 1/2 pt. — 1.99
VITAMINS 'A' AND 'C'
Fresh Asparagus — 1.29 / lb.
VITAMINS A, B, C & IRON
Green Beans — .79 / lb.
TOPS IN VITAMIN 'A'
Calif. Carrots 2 1-lb. bags — .79

Sale begins Sunday, April 1, thru Saturday, April 7 at Friendly Supermarkets of North Bergen only

❖ Exercise Four

Directions:

Read the above supermarket ad carefully. Then fill in the information below.

1. Name of supermarket chain:_____
2. Store hours:_____
3. Dates when sale prices are effective:_____
4. Location of stores where these prices are effective:_____
_____
5. How much is 1/2 gal. of Tropicana Premium Homestyle Orange Juice?
_____
6. How much is 1 lb. of ground turkey?_____
7. How much is one honeydew melon?_____
8. How much is 1 lb. of drumsticks?_____ 3 lbs.?_____
9. How much do two 8-oz. containers of sour cream cost?_____
10. How much does one 1/2 gal. of Tropicana Banana Juice cost?_____
11. How much do 4 lbs. of green beans cost?_____

SHOPPING FOR MERCHANDISE

❖ Exercise Five

Directions:

Find ads in your local newspaper for the following products.

1. An advertisement for an appliance (refrigerator, stove, toaster, microwave oven, dishwasher, etc.)

   A. Name of store:_____

   B. Location:_____

   C. Store hours (if listed):_____

   D. Phone no.:_____

E. Description of the product:_____

   _____

2. An advertisement for an audio/video product.

   A. Name of store:_____

   B. Location:_____

   C. Store hours (if listed):_____

   D. Phone no.:_____

   E. Description of the product:_____

   _____

   F. Make and model number:_____

   G. Price_____

3. An advertisement for an item of clothing.

   A. Name of store:_____

   B. Location:_____

   C. Store hours (if listed):_____

   D. Phone no.:_____

   E. Description of the product:_____

   _____

   F. Price:_____

4. An advertisement for a furniture item.

   A. Name of store:_____

   B. Location:_____

   C. Store hours (if listed):_____

   D. Phone no.:_____

   E. Description of the product:_____

   F. Price:_____

❖❖❖